P9-DDO-504

Changing Kindergartens

Four Success Stories

Editors

Stacie G. Goffin

Dolores A. Stegelin

National Association for the Education of Young Children
Washington, DC

This book is dedicated to all the unsung heroines and heroes who work on a daily basis to enrich the lives of young children through developmentally appropriate practice, because their stories may never be presented publicly.

Photo credits: pages xiii, 54, and 75/Subjects & Predicates; page 3/Don Franklin; page 6/Gail Denham; page 14/Bob Taylor; page 23/Blakely Fetridge Bundy; pages 31 and 61/Nancy P. Alexander; page 34/Lois Main; page 40/Betty C. Ford; page 47/Beth Chapote; pages 59 and 100/Jean-Claude Lejeune; page 66/Elisabeth Nichols; page 80/Larry G. Cumpton; page 85/Esther Mugar; page 91/Anne Crabbe; page 96/Robert Koenig; page 106/Elaine M. Ward.

Copyright © 1992 by Stacie G. Goffin. All rights reserved. Second printing 1993.

National Association for the Education of Young Children
1509 16th Street, N.W.
Washington, DC 20036–1426

The National Association for the Education of Young Children attempts through its publications program to provide a forum for discussion of major issues and ideas in our field. We hope to provoke thought and promote professional growth. The views expressed or implied are not necessarily those of the Association.

Cover design: Peter Masters. *Book design and production:* Betty Nylund Barr with Jack Zibulsky. *Editor:* Polly Greenberg; *Copyediting and proofreading:* Penny Atkins and Betty Nylund Barr. *Editorial assistance:* Julie Andrews.

Library of Congress Catalog Card Number: 91–067857

ISBN Catalog Number: 0–935989–49–8

NAEYC #338

Printed in the United States of America

About the Editors

Stacie G. Goffin is an associate professor of early childhood education at the University of Missouri–Kansas City. She is coauthor of *Speaking Out: Early Childhood Advocacy,* published by the National Association for the Education of Young Children, and is the author of numerous other articles and chapters. From the fall of 1988 until January 1991, she worked directly with the early childhood teachers and administrators in the Turner School District and assisted their  reconceptualization of early childhood programs. She is now actively involved with Kansas City's Metropolitan Council on Child Care and their efforts to construct a coordinated system of quality early childhood care and education in the metropolitan community.

Dolores A. Stegelin is an associate professor of early childhood education at the University of Cincinnati. She is the author of numerous professional articles on early childhood policy, public school early childhood programs, and health issues related to child care settings. Her book, *Early Childhood Education: Policy Issues for the 1990s,* is currently in press with Ablex Publishing Company. Dee was the first director of the Commonwealth of  Kentucky's first Office of Child Development in the mid-1980s, and was the primary author of their Five-Year Plan for Early Childhood Education.

About the Authors

Emily L. Murawski has taught first grade and kindergarten for most of her 20 years in education, 13 of them in the Fountain, Colorado, schools. Her teaching experiences have varied—from Spanish Harlem to Storrs, Connecticut; from Oxon Hill, Maryland, to Stockton, California. A graduate of Hunter College, she is now becoming a teacher trainer for her Colorado school district.

When her two children were young, Emily volunteered in their school and trained other school volunteers in a citywide program. A radio program by and for children that she helped to create had her writing scripts, rehearsing students, and driving the children to the radio station for weekly tapings. During a three-year stint in Alexandria, Virginia, she and two other mothers ran a science enrichment program for a private elementary school.

Nancy J. Mooney has been a speech and language therapist, learning disabilities teacher, school psychological examiner, and elementary school principal. When her chapter was written, she was the principal of Thomas Edison Elementary School in St. Joseph, Missouri. In the fall of 1991 she accepted the position of Language Arts Supervisor for the St. Joseph Public Schools. Nancy has taught more than 2,000 early

childhood teachers in summer institutes, and has provided ongoing training at the local level.

In 1988 Nancy was awarded the Early Childhood and Parent Education Distinguished Service Award by the Missouri Commissioner of Education. In 1990 she was chosen by the Missouri Elementary Principal's Association to be Missouri's National Distinguished Principal. She was later honored in Washington, D.C., as one of 60 of the nation's finest elementary administrators.

Larry May is the superintendent of the Southeast Polk Community Schools. He assumed this position on July 1, 1991. Southeast Polk Community Schools, located east of Des Moines, Iowa, is a consolidated school district of 3,500 students. During the time he authored his chapter, Larry was the assistant superintendent of Curriculum and Instruction for the Turner Unified School District in Kansas City, Kansas. He held that position from 1987 until 1991. From 1980 to 1982, and again from 1985 to 1987, he was the assistant headmaster in charge of the lower school of the American School in Rio de Janeiro. He attributes his interest in and understanding of early childhood education to this experience. Larry plans to employ a process similar to the one he used in the Turner School District in the seven elementary schools in the Southeast Polk District, where some efforts toward developmentally appropriate practices have already begun.

Although one person, Linnea Anderson, wrote Chapter 5, she shares her accomplishment with four other individuals who have been integral to the Garrett Heights Developmental Project. Pictured from left to right are Helen Atkinson, Becky Thomson, Linnea Anderson, Malissa Ruffner, and Pat Halle.

Linnea Anderson has twin daughters in second grade who completed kindergarten and first grade at Garrett Heights. Linnea is a former television anchor and is now a freelance journalist, having been a political activist in the sixties and seventies. Following her coverage of the school desegregation story in Louisville, Kentucky, she concluded that "people of all classes and races need to band together to make schools work. Courts and other institutions can only do so much."

Helen Atkinson was educated in state-run schools in Great Britain. Her mother was a preschool educator, and both of her parents believed that most education takes place outside the schools. Helen is a veteran community organizer in the areas of housing, health care, and teen pregnancy. She has come to believe that schools do, in fact, have tremendous impact on children's lives. Helen is the mother of three young sons.

Pat Halle, the mother of two young children including a third grader at Garrett Heights, received her early education at a small, coed, private school in Baltimore. "The school had this developmentally appropriate philosophy, and I guess it had a bigger impact on me than I would have thought." Halle has been a social activist since the civil rights, antiwar, and feminist movements, and now works as a paralegal, advocating for the rights of students with disabilities in the Baltimore City Public Schools.

Becky Thomson considers herself an advocate for her four children, who attend first, second, and fourth grades at Garrett Heights. She relishes her advocacy role as a parent and believes that the power to change comes from working outside the institutional system. Becky has a degree in early childhood education and has been a preschool teacher.

Malissa Ruffner is the mother of two young children, including a daughter in second grade at Garrett Heights, and is committed to urban living. With a law degree under her belt, Malissa is expanding her activism beyond Garrett Heights, doing volunteer work at an agency that is preparing a lawsuit to force equity in public school funding.

Contents

Acknowledgments

The editors acknowledge the support of the school districts and the authors who made such a commitment to sharing their personal stories about kindergarten change. We also wish to express appreciation to Polly Greenberg for recognizing the significance of these stories and the authors' efforts toward developmentally appropriate practice. We are especially grateful to our families; their support for us made this book possible.

Preface

The importance of a book on changing kindergartens stems from the current state of affairs in early childhood policy and practice. Kindergarten practices are being scrutinized because of several significant forces:

1. state and federal legislation mandating the placement of young children in public school settings and advocacy for developmentally appropriate practice for the birth-to-age-eight child population;

2. a renewed concern among educators regarding the discrepancy between current practices and the unique ways in which young children learn; and

3. new early childhood policy statements that clearly document the need for developmentally appropriate curriculum and teaching strategies with young children (e.g., Bredekamp, 1987; National Association for the Education of Young Children & National Association of Early Childhood Specialists in State Departments of Education, 1991; National Association of Elementary School Principals, 1990).

Kindergarten has been in existence for 150 years in the United States, and concerns about appropriate practice are not new. In the late 1800s and early 1900s, Froebelian kindergartens were play-oriented. They, in turn, gave way to reformation during the 1920s as part of the scientific movement. Dewey's progressive approach emerged during this time and was a forerunner of the interactionist approach to early childhood education. The 1960s, couched in the political arena of the "Great Society," produced the era of the "disadvantaged child" and the deficit approach to providing early childhood education programs, which helped propel academic content into kindergarten programs.

If hopes are realized, the current period of early childhood education will be coined "the era of developmentally appropriate practice." Supported by early childhood research that documents the value of child-initiated activity for healthy child development and NAEYC's position statement on developmentally appropriate practice (Bredekamp,

1987), national organizations and proactive groups for young children increasingly advocate a child-centered, developmentally focused learning environment and curriculum. Indeed, there seems to be a consensus among early childhood proponents that developmentally appropriate curriculum approaches are best for young children, including those who are at risk, handicapped, or developmentally delayed.

As educational reformers target early childhood education, kindergarten policy and practice has become a focal point for curricular discussions and decisions. In many ways, kindergarten education has become the new battleground for resolution of what constitutes developmentally appropriate practice within the public school early primary setting.

This book relates four experiences of individuals who have embraced the concept of developmentally appropriate practice and made the effort to translate their understandings into practice in public school settings. The primary authors of this book are a kindergarten teacher, an elementary school principal, a school superintendent, and parents of kindergarten children, each of whom tells his or her story of securing developmentally appropriate practice in kindergarten classrooms. Their stories record the humanistic, complicated process of moving from a more comfortable and traditional perspective of working with five-year-olds to an approach that demands reflection, complex implementation, and political negotiation.

It has been a privilege to work with these four authors, whom we have come to appreciate as unsung heroines and an unsung hero. At first, they doubted the significance of their stories; then they questioned their abilities to tell them; but as their stories reveal, they succeeded in retelling their personal encounters with educational change in ways that verify their success as change agents and confirm the possibility of change for children and teachers in developmentally inappropriate kindergartens.

Especially meaningful for us is the individuality of each story, even though each begins and ends in a similar fashion: with desires to see developmentally appropriate kindergarten education in their schools, and a measure of success in achieving this goal. We believe these four stories, although unique in their specifics, to be representative of the experiences of the many parents, teachers, and administrators prodding schools toward developmentally appropriate practices in kindergartens and primary grade classrooms.

These stories celebrate the efforts of individuals who have made a difference; thus, we hope they affirm the efforts of those whose stories may never receive public recognition, and inspire those still questioning their abilities to be advocates on behalf of appropriate early childhood education.

References

Bredekamp, S. (1987). *Developmentally appropriate practice in early childhood programs serving children from birth through age 8.* Washington, DC: National Association for the Education of Young Children.

National Association for the Education of Young Children & National Association of Early Childhood Specialists in State Departments of Education. (1991). Position statement: Guidelines for appropriate curriculum content and assessment in programs serving children ages 3 through 8. *Young Children, 46*(3), 21–38.

National Association of Elementary School Principals. (1990). *Early childhood education and the elementary school principal: Standards for quality programs for young children.* Alexandria, VA: Author.

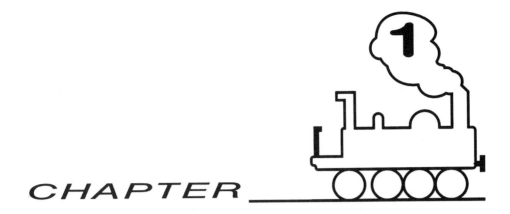

CHAPTER

Kindergarten Education: Current Policy and Practice

Dolores A. Stegelin

The purpose of this introductory chapter is to provide a context for the four focal chapters of this book. This context places kindergarten education within the larger early childhood ecosystem and identifies the specific issues that reflect the current status of kindergarten education in the United States. The term *ecosystem* is used in this chapter to mean the totality of current early childhood programs, practices, and policies. This is the larger setting within which our four authors strive to create developmentally appropriate early childhood programs. The stage is set for the stories that follow by placing them within the context of contemporary kindergarten issues in the United States.

Kindergarten within the larger early childhood ecosystem

The significance of a book on securing developmentally appropriate practice in kindergarten classrooms stems from the current state of policy in early childhood education.

1. Legislation at both the federal and state levels has mandated the expanded placement of young children into public school settings (Kagan, 1989; Mitchell & Modigliani, 1989; Stegelin, in press). Although recent policy efforts have placed considerable attention on at-risk, developmentally delayed, and handicapped children at the preschool level, legislation in many states has also focused on the need for high-quality, developmentally appropriate kindergarten classrooms (Fromberg, 1989; Glazer, 1985; Hitz & Wright, 1988; Shepard & Smith, 1986; Spodek, 1973). Indeed, within this political and educational context, early childhood educators have begun to hope that initiatives in the birth-to-five population will create a "trickle upward" of appropriate practice into the kindergarten and early elementary grades.

2. Second, the larger early childhood context includes a renewed concern among educators about how young children best learn and how they are being taught. Early childhood educators and researchers are providing convincing evidence that Americans attempt to rush their young children into premature development, subject them to unnecessary life stressors and transitions, and impose harmful early academic expectations. Recent research on the long-term benefits of early childhood education points to the value of social interaction, play, and whole-language curriculum versus teacher-directed, didactic, and skill-based curriculum approaches; thus, any description of current issues in the larger early childhood ecosystem must include the philosophical concern for what is developmentally appropriate in the provision of learning experiences for young children, including kindergarten and early elementary-age children.

3. A third driving force in early childhood education as a field is an emerging philosophical cohesiveness. During the 1980s, the field of early childhood education seemed to coalesce politically and philosophically (Kagan, 1989). One of the central forces bringing the field together was the collective realization that young children learn in ways that are best facilitated by hands-on, constructivist teaching approaches (Bredekamp, 1987). Because kindergarten has been in existence for over 150 years in the United States (Spodek, 1988), this concern for how young children learn is obviously not new but is fueled and broadened by the

recent legislative mandates that target the comprehensive birth-to-five early childhood population.

Looking back over the past two decades, this period in early childhood education is marked by dramatic political, fiscal, and educational growth. The field has broadened and is now clearly defined as the entire birth-to-age-eight child population; but although new subpopulations have been identified, both for educational and administrative purposes, kindergarten is still a vanguard of early childhood education in the United States and enjoys its own growing visibility and continued evolution within the field.

Other variables that must be considered when studying the entire fabric of early childhood education, which of course includes kindergarten issues, are the intense public scrutiny of our nation's educational system as a whole, the conclusion that the United States lags behind other countries in such areas as math and science education, and the subsequent fervor for educational reform that pervades the United States. Along with the public's concern for performance has come an enlarged emphasis on testing and standardized achievement scores, even for young children (see also Kamii, 1989). These two factors—educational accountability and standardized testing—account for much of the new emphasis on academic readiness now being placed on kindergarten children. Historically, kindergarten has enjoyed a separate status, even within the public school scenario (Spodek, 1988). With the recent emphasis on academic preparation and school readiness, however, the traditional separation of kindergarten, with its greater emphasis on play as a primary vehicle of learning, has given way to the inclusion of kindergarten as a more integral part of the early elementary years, along with a more traditional academic focus.

Thus, the current mosaic of early childhood programs and issues has been expanded dramatically by the policy initiatives of the 1980s. Legislative mandates have defined new early childhood populations and have expanded our definition of early education. New emphasis is placed on at-risk and developmentally delayed child populations. Also instrumental in creating the current status of the field are initiatives in two areas: educational reform and standardized testing.

As we move toward the 21st century, we are at a major new crossroads in kindergarten education. While develop-

Dolores A. Stegelin

mentalists have endeavored to include the kindergarten child as part of the early childhood population (along with the primary grades) and to advocate for developmentally appropriate learning settings in kindergarten, traditional early childhood educational practices are being challenged by those who advocate for academic success, school readiness, standardized testing, and the inclusion of kindergarten classrooms in those efforts. Educational reform across the country paints a mixed picture of kindergarten education; some states are developing kindergarten policy that is reflective of developmentally appropriate practice, while others define the kindergarten population within the confines of the larger elementary school. Clearly, kindergarten issues are at the forefront of the great educational reform debate and represent an enlarged and broadened philosophical struggle between the developmentalists on one hand and the academic/school readiness advocates on the other. The kindergarten classroom appears to be a fertile new battleground for these philosophical differences.

Current kindergarten issues

Kindergarten education in the United States has become universal for the majority of the nation's five-year-olds. Approximately 95% of all five-year-olds attend some type of kindergarten program (Sava, 1987). Each September, more than three million children begin formal schooling with their first day of kindergarten (Shepard & Smith, 1986); thus, the kindergarten scenario affects many children. Fromberg (1989) describes the current kindergarten arena as a variety of paradigms for kindergarten programming, growing out of different views of what is developmentally appropriate, how young children learn, and what teaching strategies are worthwhile.

Policy trends in kindergarten during the 1980s and the emerging 1990s address the following issues:

1. school entry age and readiness;

2. the use of screening tests to determine readiness;

3. the rapidly rising rate of kindergarten failure; and

4. the growing use of narrowly defined kindergarten curricula that seem to focus more on academic skills than

on developmentally appropriate activities (Freeman, 1990; Peck, McCaig, & Sapp, 1988; Shepard & Smith, 1986; Walsh, 1989). In addition, elementary schools are adding pre-first grade classes in an effort to address the readiness and failure issues. These new classes have many names, but typically are referred to as prekindergarten and transitional first grade (Walsh, 1989).

Freeman (1990) presents the central theme that brings all the issues together most comprehensively: What does it mean to be ready for kindergarten? (See also National Association for the Education of Young Children, 1990.) Within this broader theme are included the more specific issues of entrance age, school readiness, testing and screening concerns, appropriate curriculum for the five-year-old, and the appropriateness of adding "new" classes prior to the first grade. Also included in this theme is the fundamental definition and concept of *developmental appropriateness.* Walsh (1989) argues that current kindergarten practice, particularly related to screening and assessment, is based more on an older, outdated, maturational definition of child development rather than the more current and accepted interactionist interpretation.

What are the current needs for kindergarten practice and policy? These needs include research-based information for decision making about the issue of readiness and the use of appropriate screening and assessment instruments, current child development and theory-based curriculum, more awareness and involvement on the part of kindergarten parents, advocacy at all levels (including public school administrators, teachers, and other school-based personnel), and decision making based on the needs of the specific state and community. This latter concept is a part of *site-based management,* a popular term in current educational reform circles.

One concern among kindergarten advocates is that educational reform and policy change have swept the country suddenly and comprehensively in many states (Kentucky, my home state, is an example). Possibly lacking in this policy development process is sufficient time for reflection about the specific needs of a particular community or state before educational reform policy is passed and implemented. What may be appropriate for rural Kentucky may not be appropriate for urban Philadelphia. In this time of educational reform, early childhood advocates would do well to slow down the pace of grand scale reform efforts. Rather than blanket acceptance of policy and practice as established in other states, early childhood advocates should encourage the development of site-specific kindergarten policy and practice.

Within this broader context of early childhood education practice and policy, and with specific kindergarten education issues in mind, the four chapters that follow describe the site-specific efforts of four "reformers": Emily, a teacher; Nancy, a principal; Larry, a superintendent; and Linnea, a parent. As a group, they represent the core collaborators in any successful implementation of developmentally appropriate practice in kindergarten classrooms. As individuals, they represent the cast of players whose personal stories can provide valuable insight to others in parallel positions.

On a personal note

My role as a child development professional has evolved steadily over two decades. The ideas and attitudes that I bring to kindergarten issues are shaped by those experiences. I therefore begin with a brief personal and professional introduction, followed by an overview of the current early childhood ecosystem and a focused examination of the specific subsystem within early childhood education known as *kindergarten education.*

My roots in early education

As my fellow editor and I worked with the authors of the four stories that follow, I found myself reflecting on my own personal and professional experiences as they relate to kindergarten. Although I hold graduate degrees in child development and early childhood education, have been a classroom teacher, and consider myself to be multifaceted as a teacher educator, researcher, practitioner, policymaker, and advocate, I found that my connections with early education go back to my childhood roots.

Having grown up on the plains of Kansas on a 400-acre dairy farm and having attended a one-room country school with never more than 15 students and 1 teacher (with an occasional parent volunteer) allows me to bring a fresh, personal view of school-starting experiences. My first school experience was in the first grade (a kindergarten curriculum was still being established), where I quickly learned the value of individualized teaching (there were only three students in my grade!), the wonders and excitement of books and print, and the doors of knowledge that the printed word opened. This rural Kansas setting promoted a feeling of pioneer exploration and self-discovery, providing rich memories of my first school experience.

My earliest recollection of going to elementary school was that learning was a daily adventure, often beginning with a two-mile walk to the school or, alternatively, a bumpy ride on our old black horse. Early schooling for me was filled with individual learning experiences; intimate, small-group interactions; and large-group, multiage activities related to games and outdoor routines such as softball, tag, and relay races. The white schoolhouse was located on about five acres of land with many trees and a barn and an old country cemetery adjacent to the school grounds. Every day was different, and, for the most part, it was positive. The children were friends, as were most of their families, and going to school was an integral part of daily living. Sharing was inherent in the early school routine—shared indoor and outdoor tasks, shared reading and writing experiences, shared tutoring and peer assistance, and a shared sense of community. Somehow we all knew who we were and how we fit into that school's small but cohesive culture. There was a pronounced sense of belonging and investment in the learning process. Many of my early learning experiences were developmentally appropriate, even though the term had not yet been coined.

Teaching and learning were personalized experiences—personalized by the teacher, personalized by students in the same grade, and personalized by older peers who nurtured my early intellectual growth. There was sufficient time to share feelings and to convey concerns (one example being the noon hours when we sat together on the cement porch, like an extended family, to eat lunches from our sundry lunchboxes and brown paper bags and to converse about the daily events of home, school, and the immediate community). Perhaps it was this personalization and sense of community that mediated those teaching and learning experiences that were less appropriate for the younger students, and perhaps it is the lack of those mediating factors that contributes to the sense of anonymity and disconnectedness that characterizes so many classrooms today.

Contrasting yesterday with today

The early schooling that I experienced in that rural Kansas setting was a far cry from early schooling today and what has evolved in kindergarten education over the past two decades.

My own children, ages 12 and 18, attended kindergarten settings that are more reflective of our current educational times. Although both of them initially experienced developmental kindergartens, my son (who has a late-September birthday) is also the product of a transitional first grade. As parents, my husband and I experienced the traumas sometimes associated with the decision making related to transitional classes and processes.

My professional experiences include involvement in early childhood policy development and implementation. As the first director of the Commonwealth of Kentucky's first Office of Child Development in the mid-1980s, I participated in early legislative efforts that led to recent educational reform in that state; thus I am sensitive to the critical balance that must exist between sound policy and appropriate practice.

My current professional responsibility as a teacher educator takes me into diverse and philosophically inconsistent public preschool and kindergarten classrooms in a large, urban, midwestern city where "educational reform" is on the tip of everyone's tongue. As I read the current literature on kindergarten education across the United States, consider my children's experiences, and reflect on my own atypical early schooling experience, I am struck by the rapidity of change in kindergarten practice in just my lifetime.

As a teacher educator and researcher in the area of public school early childhood education, I am fascinated by the ever-changing mosaic of programs and initiatives labeled *early childhood education.*

Suggested reading for early childhood teacher educators

Elkind, D. (1987). *Miseducation: Preschoolers at risk.* New York: Alfred A. Knopf, Inc.

Meisels, S. J. (1989). *Developmental screening in early childhood: A guide* (3rd. ed.). Washington, DC: National Association for the Education of Young Children.

Shepard, L. A., & Smith, M. L. (1988). Escalating academic demand in kindergarten: Some nonsolutions. *The Elementary School Journal, 89,* 135–146.

Spodek, B. (1988). Conceptualizing today's kindergarten curriculum. *The Elementary School Journal, 89,* 203–212.

References

Bredekamp, S. (Ed.). (1987). *Developmentally appropriate practice in early childhood programs serving children from birth through age 8* (exp. ed.). Washington, DC: National Association for the Education of Young Children.

Freeman, E. B. (1990). Issues in kindergarten policy and practice. *Young Children, 55*(4), 29–34.

Fromberg, D. (1989). Kindergarten: Current circumstances affecting curriculum. *Teachers College Record, 90,* 393–403.

Glazer, J. (1985). Kindergarten and early education. *Childhood Education, 62,* 13–18.

Hitz, R., & Wright, D. (1988). Kindergarten issues: A practitioner's survey. *Principal, 67,* 28–30.

Kagan, S. (1989). Early care and education: Tackling the tough issues. *Phi Delta Kappan, 70,* 433–439.

Kamii, C. (Ed.). (1990). *Achievement testing in the early grades: The games grown-ups play.* Washington, DC: National Association for the Education of Young Children.

Mitchell, A., & Modigliani, K. (1989). Young children in public schools? The "only ifs" reconsidered. *Young Children, 44*(6), 56–61.

National Association for the Education of Young Children. (1990). NAEYC position statement on school readiness. *Young Children, 46*(1), 21–23.

Peck, J. T., McCaig, C., & Sapp, M. E. (1988). *Kindergarten policies: What is best for children?* Washington, DC: National Association for the Education of Young Children.

Sava, S. G. (1987). Development, not readiness. *Young Children, 42*(5), 15.

Shepard, L., & Smith, M. (1986). Synthesis of research on school readiness and kindergarten retention. *Educational Leadership, 44,* 78–86.

Spodek, B. (1973). Needed: A new view of kindergarten education. *Childhood Education, 49,* 191–196.

Spodek, B. (1988). Conceptualizing today's kindergarten curriculum. *The Elementary School Journal, 89,* 196–203.

Stegelin, D. A. (in press). *Early childhood education: Policy issues for the 1990s.* Norwood, NJ: Ablex Publishing Co.

Walsh, D. (1989). Changes in kindergarten: Why here? Why now? *Early Childhood Research Quarterly, 4,* 377–391.

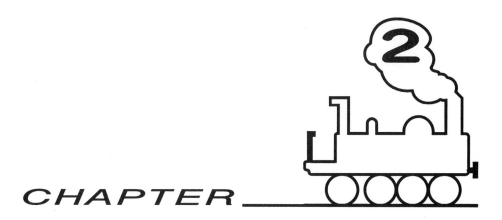

CHAPTER

Changing Kindergartens: Teachers as Change Agents

Emily L. Murawski

This is the story of kindergarten teachers creating change in a small school district south of Colorado Springs, Colorado. In Fountain–Fort Carson School District, 3,500 students attend five elementary schools, two middle schools, and one high school. Two of the elementary schools and one middle school are on a large Army post, Fort Carson, where student turnover approaches 60% annually.

There are 354 kindergartners who attend our half-day sessions. They're taught by nine full-time teachers, who daily teach two sessions, and two part-time teachers, who each teach one session.

I've taught first grade or kindergarten for most of my 20 years in the classroom, across six states and seven school districts. Before my husband retired from the Air Force, we moved every few years, leaving the Fountain area several times but always coming back. Because I changed everything from curtains to classrooms so often, it was inevitable that I'd change the way I teach.

How my teaching has changed

When I started teaching in 1964, kindergarten was different from the other primary grades (first and second grade). It focused on children's interests and their developmental levels. Classroom life was child centered. In the other primary grades, we focused on dispensing blocks of knowledge. In my first grade classroom, life was curriculum centered.

Since then, much of the first grade curriculum has trickled down to kindergarten. It isn't unusual for kindergarten children to do many pencil-and-paper tasks, such as working in phonics workbooks, filling in squares on worksheets, and even taking standardized tests. And ditto sheets—they're everywhere.

In moving from teaching first grade to teaching kindergarten in 1978, I drew heavily on my experiences with first grade. And yes, I brought along my share of dittos, in an effort to give my kindergartners what I considered a challenging curriculum; but my kindergarten teaching wasn't grounded in a knowledge of how young children learn. I had taken no child development courses in college and, like most busy teachers, I hadn't kept up with the research.

I started to change the way I teach kindergarten in 1985, during my year with the city schools in Alexandria, Virginia. I had the good fortune to work with some former preschool teachers who brought their early childhood insights to kindergarten education. They promoted developmentally appropriate practices by leading informal meetings with district kindergarten teachers. They also alerted me to a terrific state-sponsored conference on kindergarten, and the school district sponsored my attendance.

These experiences gave me the confidence to change. I abandoned my reliance on textbooks and moved to thematic approaches for teaching language arts, social studies, and science. I started to use a strong manipulative approach to teaching mathematics, and I stopped feeling guilty about including free play.

When I returned to Colorado in 1986, I was a believer in developmentally appropriate practice. I had joined the National Association for the Education of Young Children, increased my reading of early childhood research, and resolved to further improve my teaching.

How NOT to create change

Although I returned to a school in which I had taught years earlier, the homecoming was frustrating. I shared a classroom with a kindergarten teacher whose methods were much different from mine. When I arrived, the classroom had no toys. The playhouse furniture gathered dust in the cafeteria closet, and the workbench held the DDD (daily dose of dittos). In contrast, I needed activity areas, space for manipulatives, and lots of books for the classroom library.

The morning teacher and I eventually made some strained compromises. I added my activity centers to the room, for example, while she kept her rigid seating arrangement.

I fared no better with the other two kindergarten teachers. I declined their well-intentioned offers of dittos, saying, "My children aren't ready for them." But my politeness didn't disguise my disapproval. They took my view of their methods personally, and I found myself isolated. Even announcements of grade-level meetings somehow didn't reach me.

Although well meaning, the novice principal knew too little about early childhood education to support me, and he was preoccupied with his many other tasks. He wanted his kindergarten teachers to get along, but our philosophies and teaching strategies differed too widely.

I felt so frustrated. I knew that either the other kindergarten teachers had to change or I had to leave. After a year, I chose to transfer to another school. I needed a more hospitable place to work, and my husband was getting tired of my complaints.

At that time I thought of myself not as an agent of change but as a teacher trying to do a good job. I threatened the comfortable and easy ways of my colleagues. I realize now that I should have worked at sharing research with them and accepting some of their offers. I should have cultivated their trust. I should have tried to persuade them toward practicing in a more developmentally appropriate way.

Better chemistry elsewhere

Things improved when I moved to a newly opened school in the district. This school had 350 students, about half the number at the school I had just left. Students came from the modest suburban community in which the school was located and from the surrounding rural area, where small houses and trailers dotted the prairie. Most important, I could work with Jan Koester, the other half-time kindergarten teacher. Her approach to teaching young children was more like mine.

I could also work with the principal, Dr. Bill Weeks. He admitted to knowing little about early childhood education. Similar to many elementary principals, his background was in secondary education, yet he convinced us that he wanted to learn. So Jan and I began educating him with a steady stream of articles. Eventually, Dr. Weeks started sending articles to us, with notes such as, "Have you ever heard of Lilian Katz?"

Dr. Weeks recognized that Jan and I were on to something. He bought us new materials and sent us to conferences. When talking with the other four elementary principals and the superintendent, he promoted what "his" kindergartens were doing. A vocal advocate, Dr. Weeks helped make developmentally appropriate practice politically legitimate. By the time teachers pressed for broad acceptance of developmentally appropriate practice two years later, the superintendent and the building principals would be more open to our ideas.

Getting good at developmentally appropriate practice

At this point, Jan and I experimented with developmentally appropriate practice in our classrooms. We bought a sand-and-water table, for example, where children made styrofoam boats, experimented with floating and sinking objects, and made a volcano in which to bury their plastic dinosaurs.

We integrated the curriculum. When we studied community helpers, we took field trips, wrote experience stories, and role played. After visiting a fire station, children wrote stories and drew illustrations about the trip, created a list of fire safety rules, and converted the playhouse into their own fire station. At the same time, the children studied the letters *F* and *S*. They wrote the letters, learned their sounds, and cooked foods beginning with those letters. Creating a class store actively involved children in learning about money, and they created signs and price tags, wrote bills for customers, counted pennies, and made change.

The children also had their own post office. After visiting a real one, we set up a post office in the classroom. Children sold stamps, canceled stamps on letters they wrote at the writing center, sorted letters by address, and delivered them to individual mailboxes in the classroom.

Our integrated approach benefited children, teachers, and parents. Children were interested and were *learning*. With so many things going on in this new classroom, "problem" children suddenly seemed less disruptive. Those we might previously have labeled as "learning disabled" were now able to find things they could do successfully.

First grade teachers reported that our students performed as well academically as students taught in more conventional ways, while their interest in reading and writing seemed greater. One first grade teacher told me that when something special occurred, our former students would frequently ask, "Can we write a story about it?"

Parents were pleased to see their children enthusiastic about school. This reflected, in part, their understanding of my classroom goals. During the first two days of school, children come in one at a time with their parents to meet me. They also spend 20 minutes exploring the room, choosing a cubby, and investigating the classroom materials. During this time, I tell parents about my teaching philosophy and provide an article on how young children learn. I also enlist parent volunteers. Although the number of volunteers is small because so many mothers and fathers are employed, the volunteers indirectly serve as advocates of developmentally appropriate practice with other parents.

For two years, with Jan's support, I concentrated on making my own teaching more developmentally appropriate and sharing new information with the principal. Like so many teachers, however, I worked in isolation from those in other buildings. Except for rumors, I knew little about kindergarten practices elsewhere.

Discovering a mood for change

The opportunity to influence kindergarten practices in other buildings came in the fall of 1988, when the district's curriculum director asked grade-level teachers to meet and write the district's mathematics objectives and choose its mathematics books.

When kindergarten teachers met, their discussion returned again and again to issues they believed the district needed to resolve before they could settle on math objectives or texts. According to teachers, a worrisome number of kindergartners and first graders were being retained because the children weren't ready to move on. Should the district avoid retaining children in kindergarten by creating transitional first grades? There was also the curriculum director's recent decision to administer the Iowa Test of Basic Skills to all first and second graders. Was such early testing wise?

These same concerns arose in meetings of first and second grade teachers. Knowing that changes in one grade would affect others, Pam Young, a highly respected first grade teacher, invited kindergarten, first grade, and second grade teachers to a get-together in her room to learn each others' views. This effort was informal: One teacher simply called another. We didn't think to invite principals, and we had no specific agenda.

During our discussion, there was talk of solving the retention problem by having students start school when they were a little older. It was argued that older children would be more mature and ready to accept our curriculum. I and others argued, instead, for changing the curriculum to fit the needs of children. Many of our students came from low-income families in which there are few experiences conducive to school success. Our teaching, not children's starting age, needed to change.

This informal meeting was a breakthrough. The feeling in the room was that something was amiss in the way we were teaching young children. The talk turned to *developmentally appropriate practice,* even though many of the teachers didn't know the term. Jan and I *did* know the term, however, and so did Yevonne Conrad, the district's only teacher with a degree in early childhood education. Together, we started selling a better way to teach kindergarten.

Yevonne and I sent research articles to the kindergarten, first grade, and second grade teachers in all five elementary schools, as well as to the district curriculum director. The research (Shepard & Smith, 1986; 1987) showed that children who repeated kindergarten or attended transitional first grades had higher dropout rates.

Other research explained that standardized testing of children younger than age eight was suspect. These findings, of course, directly challenged the proposal to administer the Iowa Test of Basic Skills to all first and second graders. Overall, the research supported moving to a developmentally appropriate program.

The district curriculum director, however, remained distant from our efforts. She seemed uninterested in developmentally appropriate practice and explained her stance by contending, "The superintendent doesn't like developmental." Yevonne and I continued to keep her informed, but realized that we would have to take the lead. Fortunately, she never thwarted our efforts and eventually even provided the opportunity that permitted us to publicly share our views with the superintendent and building principals.

This opportunity occurred when the curriculum director, in response to our persistence, asked Yevonne to write a report for district administrators and kindergarten teachers on the relevance of early childhood research to teaching. Fearing that no one would read such a report, Yevonne and I offered to make an oral presentation, and the curriculum director acquiesced.

Despite the curriculum director's declaration that the superintendent was opposed to developmental practice, we suspected that he simply had little understanding of the concept. We hoped that the presentation would be our chance to inform the district's top trendsetter about developmentally appropriate practice and to win his support.

Briefing the superintendent

The curriculum director invited the superintendent and the elementary principals to our presentation in early March. Yevonne and I sent our own invitations to all the primary teachers. The after-school presentation was well attended. The superintendent, Dr. Michael Martin, was present, and so were three of the five elementary principals, the curriculum director, some first and second grade teachers, and most kindergarten teachers. The 45-minute presentation had three parts:

1. an overview of Piaget's stages of cognitive development (Pulaski, 1980, was our resource for this information) and the latest research on teaching young children, supported by overhead transparencies and handouts;

Emily L. Murawski

2. a 10-minute videotape made by Jan Koester, showing kindergartners and first graders in our building involved with developmentally appropriate activities: using a wide variety of manipulatives for math, building a structure in the block area, role playing in a housekeeping area, using language experience stories to learn language arts, and dictating a story typed at a classroom computer center by a sixth grader;

3. a proposal for making the district's kindergarten and first grades more developmentally appropriate. Our main thrust was toward educating teachers and administrators. Specifically, primary teachers would start a study group—the Primary Council—to become experts in developmentally appropriate practice.

During the 45 minutes of discussion that followed, the talk quickly turned to how developmentally appropriate practice might affect standardized test scores among first and second graders. The district was trying to raise its standards, using standardized test scores as a major measure. There was even talk that the state legislature might somehow tie funding to test scores.

Yevonne and I didn't know the exact relationship between developmentally appropriate practice and test scores—only that standardized testing of children younger than age eight was unreliable. We offered alternative ways to measure progress: portfolios of student work, observations, and teacher-made tests.

Perhaps because the discussion didn't resolve the testing issue, the meeting ended without closure. Standardized testing was still a worry. The superintendent complimented us on our presentation, but didn't commit himself to our cause. What did his silence mean?

Although the presentation itself had been a success, Yevonne and I feared that the discussion on testing had overshadowed our larger purpose. If only we had anticipated the testing issue and had researched the subject more fully.

Perseverance pays off

To get closure, Yevonne and I persevered. We requested a meeting with the superintendent. At this meeting, we received his permission to form the Primary Council (description to follow) and to educate the administration about early childhood issues. There was no lack of commitment now. That afternoon in late March 1989, teachers were empowered to create change.

Just days after our meeting with the superintendent, *Newsweek* published a sympathetic cover story on early childhood education (Kantrowitz & Wingert, 1989). We took advantage of our luck and sent the article to the superintendent. Lo and behold, portions appeared in his weekly newsletter to staff and in his monthly newsletter to parents . . . along with his endorsement of our ideas. There for all to see was support from the top!

Later in the spring of 1989, when the district's kindergarten teachers voted on mathematics textbooks, the majority rejected *all* textbooks for mathematics and adopted "Math Their Way," a manipulatives program based on Piaget's levels of cognitive development. First and second grade teachers also chose this program to supplement their texts.

For the few kindergarten teachers who couldn't—or wouldn't —let go of textbook teaching, the curriculum director bought a teacher's guide and resource kit for a math series. Even though the kit consisted of too many dittos, it at least included good ideas for manipulatives.

That summer, the district held workshops for teachers to learn how to use a manipulative math program. Principals expected all kindergarten teachers to attend, and they did. In those workshops, as well as in later ones, many participants have come from grades one and two. The kindergarten movement is spreading.

Looking back, I'm glad Yevonne and I persevered. We sought deeper improvements than just raising the admission age or establishing transitional first grades. And when we ran into resistance, we didn't give up.

Studying and selling developmentally appropriate practice

Today, developmentally appropriate practice has an established teacher base in the Primary Council. The impetus for this teacher group was the uneasiness over practices that was voiced at the grade-level meetings on mathematics objectives and textbooks. Teachers wanted a forum for learning new techniques and making changes in the district.

Emily L. Murawski

Because Yevonne and I suggested such a group in our presentation to the superintendent, others looked to us to get it going. We started in May 1989, with a flier to all primary teachers and an organizational meeting to learn the teachers' interests and to establish meeting times.

The Primary Council meets about every six weeks during the school year and once during the summer months. We have a historian to keep a scrapbook that documents our meetings. About half of the primary teachers and a few elementary administrators attend regularly. Sites for the meeting rotate among the five elementary schools, and this helps to spread the word. Invariably, building administrators attend when their building hosts the meeting. Topics for meetings come from suggestions made by teachers in the district's annual staff development survey. Yevonne and I then locate speakers.

Primary Council meetings have included

• two free-lance reading specialists who talked about the whole-language approach;

• a preschool director who explained the link between the preschool and public schools;

• a field trip to Denver to observe a High/Scope kindergarten;

• a local college professor who talked about ways to make reading instruction more developmentally appropriate; and

• ten teachers who described the developmentally appropriate projects for which they had successfully secured grants.

Administrators pay attention to the Primary Council. The superintendent advertised our first meeting in his weekly staff newsletter and attended several meetings himself—strong signals to other administrators. All administrators receive invitations to meetings and copies of research articles.

This activism has helped promote developmentally appropriate practice with the principal whose school I left several years ago. He recently hired a new kindergarten teacher who is an early childhood specialist. This fall, the principal attended the NAEYC conference and sent his three kindergarten teachers to a whole-language conference in Denver.

To promote candor among teachers, however, we want to keep some distance from the administration; so, for example, the Primary Council declined a request by the curriculum director to overhaul the K–2 report cards. We did not want to become an arm of the administration. We also believed that the task would be better handled by a formal committee rather than the Primary Council.

In the 18 months the Primary Council has existed, developmentally appropriate practice has gone from being virtually unknown in the district to being a widely accepted concept. Not surprisingly, some of our five elementary schools are closer to the concept than others. In one school, developmentally appropriate practice is spotty. In my school, all kindergarten, first grade, and second grade teachers use it.

Work remains

The district has made progress toward resolving the big issues that first surfaced in 1988 in our grade-level meetings. The admission age has remained the same: All children who are five years old by September 15 may come to school. Teachers have stopped pushing for transitional first grades, often opting instead for developmentally appropriate practice. Persuaded by the research, the superintendent ended standardized testing of first graders. Although second graders continue to take the Iowa Tests of Basic Skills, I'm hopeful that this policy will also be changed.

I think the district now needs to formally declare that developmentally appropriate practice is its philosophy for the primary grades; then everyone will be aiming in the same direction. In the meantime, it is the Primary Council that keeps primary teachers and principals focused on that target.

We also need the district to fund more in-service education opportunities by child development specialists. Our new curriculum director, who began in the fall of 1990, has an early childhood education background and supports staff development. She has provided funds for the Primary Council to pay its speakers, but our meetings are too short for in-depth training. Important, too, is additional money to send more teachers to conferences.

It is also time for teachers other than Yevonne and me to run the Primary Council. We need to persuade other teachers to arrange meetings and keep administrators current on early childhood issues. New leadership will help spread change; besides, Yevonne and I are thinking about other issues . . . .

We're just beginning to educate parents about developmentally appropriate practice. Even though the district has long encouraged parent volunteers in classrooms, last year, kindergarten and first grade teachers in my building went further. We held a primary math night to explain to parents how their children learn through manipulatives and how they could help their children at home. This year we're adding a session for parents on the whole-language approach to reading.

Finally, just when things were changing, the superintendent moved on. We worry about whether Dr. Martin's replacement will share his inclination to drop standardized testing for the first and second grade. Will the new superintendent permit teachers to take risks by trying new things? Will he continue to pay for staff development to train our teachers in developmentally appropriate practice? Will he hire early childhood specialists to teach primary grades? As my building's representative on the committee that interviewed prospective superintendents, I asked these questions out loud this past summer. Although I was satisfied with the incoming superintendent's views on developmentally appropriate practice, his support is untested. The challenges to practicing in developmentally appropriate ways never end. It's always something.

Advice on creating change

To foster change, it helps to stumble into the right place at the right time, but that's just luck. To make the most of that luck, I've learned this:

• Look for allies early on. It's too hard—and probably less effective—to be a lone ranger.

• Work for broad support. Educate your opponents if you can; go around them if you must. Sparring wastes time.

• Remember that research support is good, but administrative support is better.

• Understand that most administrators know little about early childhood education. You have to educate them.

• Keep the faith. Individuals and institutions change slowly and unevenly. Those who need to change the most may accept change the least. But improvement *is* possible!

Emily L. Murawski

Postscript . . . one year later

Positive changes have continued to occur during the past year. The new superintendent discontinued the use of the Iowa Tests of Basic Skills for our second graders. As a result, many primary teachers have begun to keep portfolios, which provide a fuller record of student progress.

Although the district still lacks a parent-education program of its own, progress has been made. The local Army post's Child Development Center is beginning a pilot program that is open to all interested parents of children in our school district. These sessions will be led by early childhood educators and a psychologist. Our district is providing support by opening its schools, on and off the post, to this program, and by offering the help of the district's preschool teachers.

Developmentally appropriate practice fits well into the sweeping educational restructuring begun by our new superintendent. A cadre of 28 teachers and administrators is preparing to train the rest of the district's faculty in research-proven strategies that range from inductive thinking and concept attainment to cooperative learning and synectics (a strategy for higher order thinking). Practitioners of developmentally appropriate practice are comfortable using these strategies in their classrooms because they enable children to take greater control of their learning.

Finally, Primary Council meetings continue to draw approximately 25 progressive teachers from prekindergarten classrooms through second grade. At our last meeting, several kindergarten teachers floated the idea of seeking NAEYC accreditation—a sign of how far some of us have come in the past year.

Readings that helped us in our effort

Bredekamp, S. (Ed.). (1987). *Developmentally appropriate practice in early childhood programs serving children from birth through age 8.* Washington, DC: National Association for the Education of Young Children.

Elkind, D. (1981). *The hurried child: Growing up too fast, too soon.* Reading, MA: Addison-Wesley.

Kamii, C. (Ed.). (1990). *Achievement testing in the early grades: The games grown-ups play.* Washington, DC: National Association for the Education of Young Children.

Kantrowitz, B., & Wingert, P. (1989, April). How kids learn. *Newsweek,* pp. 50–56.

Pulaski, M. A. S. (1980). *Understanding Piaget: An introduction to children's cognitive development.* New York: Harper & Row.

Shepard, L. A., & Smith, M. L. (1986). Synthesis of research on school readiness and kindergarten retention. *Educational Leadership, 44*(3), 78–86.

Shepard, L. A., & Smith, M. L. (1987). Effects of kindergarten retention at the end of first grade. *Psychology in the Schools, 24,* 346–357.

Suggested reading for kindergarten teachers

Katz, L. G., & Chard, S. C. (1988). *Engaging children's minds: The Project Approach.* Norwood, NJ: Ablex.

Krogh, S. (1990). *The integrated early childhood curriculum.* New York: McGraw Hill.

McKee, J. S., & Thibault, J. P. (1982). Practical parenting with Piaget. *Young Children, 38*(1), 18–27.

CHAPTER

Coming To Know:
A Principal's Story

Nancy J. Mooney

My journey toward understanding early childhood education, appropriate practices, and developmental theory has spanned almost 10 years. During this period I have also become increasingly involved in promoting appropriate practices in early childhood public school programs. My story is as much a tale of personal growth as one of leadership in promoting appropriate early childhood programs. Based upon my own growth in understanding the constructive nature of learning, I can appreciate the support needed by others willing to take a similar journey. The growth of appropriate early childhood education at Edison Elementary School clearly parallels my own.

In the beginning—Extensive exposure and training

I was first introduced to the notion of early childhood education in August 1981 when an associate superintendent in the St. Joseph, Missouri, School District asked me to represent the district in a project initiated by the Missouri Department of Elementary and Secondary Education (DESE). Fifteen pilot sites were being selected to serve as demonstration preschool classrooms for Missouri's first public school programs. As part of the project, fifteen individuals were being identified by DESE for training with the High/Scope Educational Foundation on the use of the Cognitively Oriented Curriculum. It could have been a different demonstration project (as long as it was still constructivist in orientation); what matters to my story is that my state department of education established a cluster of pilot developmentally appropriate early childhood education classrooms and involved a number of the state's professional educators in the project on an intensive and extensive basis.

The Training of Trainers course taught by the High/Scope Foundation was spread over a seven-month period, which included a week of training each month followed by three weeks of attempts to implement what had been learned. The group of 15 people quickly became a network of support for each other as we struggled to understand a different interpretation of the learning process and tried to apply it to the real world of public school education. Regardless of the chosen curriculum framework, an effective strategy in promoting change is the concept of demonstration classes and a considerable amount of exposure to them followed by discussion on the part of a number of practitioners who can support each other as they struggle to understand and implement new ideas.

From behaviorist to Piagetian

Truly, I was one of the group's worst skeptics. My background and training in speech correction and practice as a public school therapist were heavily entrenched in behaviorism. In addition, my master's degree was in learning disabilities and, at the time of this special training, I was employed as a diagnostic consultant. My job administering intelligence and achievement tests and conducting and reporting on staffing with teachers and administrators to determine a child's need for special education reinforced my behavioristic leanings. Except for my organizational skills and experience with teaching teachers, I was a poor match with the philosophy of developmentally appropriate early childhood education.

Little by little, however, what we read and discussed made sense. By the time we talked about Piaget's ideas regarding disequilibrium, assimilation, and accommodation, I had a

real sense of what they meant in terms of my own learning. This was a time of metamorphosis for me, a change from behaviorist to Piagetian theorist through—in my particular case—the framework of the High/Scope curriculum.

This personal metamorphosis, and that of my colleagues, helped me to understand that individuals "come to know" and understand developmental theory and practices from many perspectives. People from many different backgrounds can embrace early childhood education and practice it effectively. The most important thing is to be a learner, which I continue to be to this day.

Getting started

Meanwhile, in St. Joseph, the process of implementing a preschool classroom was an ongoing pressure. I would return after each week's training fired up with enthusiasm only to find a week's worth of work on my desk and few sympathetic ears. Although administrators were glad that I was learning and were pleased with my enthusiasm for the project, they were more interested in details of program administration than in undertanding the theory that was fast becoming a consuming part of my thinking.

Selecting good early childhood education teachers

In January 1982, a facility and a teacher for the preschool were chosen. Thomas Edison School, where I later became principal, was selected as the demonstration site.

Edison School is a Chapter 1 school in the middle of the city of St. Joseph, Missouri, population 80,000. The teacher, Geneva Snapp, was a former kindergarten teacher who possessed both the desire and the inclination to begin this project. We met and discussed the rather awesome task ahead and formed a bond that lasts to this day.

The district agreed to hire a substitute for Geneva for two school days, and I was charged to pass on to Geneva in those two days what I had been learning over several months. I had seen High/Scope classrooms but never actually taught one. I had knowledge of four-year-olds but no experience with them as an educator. Geneva, however, brought with her a rich background of kindergarten experiences, intuitive knowledge of young children's development, and perseverance. During those two days we held long discussions, watched films, and made plans for the room's arrangement, the daily routine, and materials and equipment.

This first classroom was funded by Chapter 1 and was designed as preschool education for four-year-olds with delayed development according to Chapter 1 criteria. When the process of recruiting children began, I naively believed that everyone would be as excited about public preschool education as Geneva and I. The process of informing parents and encouraging their children's participation was slow and frequently discouraging, however; it required explaining and defending over and over the philosophy of the curriculum and the details of the program.

Giving support and promoting teachers and their new practices

Although the staff at Edison were reasonably curious about the new program, the preschool and its teacher were frequently overlooked in schoolwide functions. I was fortunate to be the diagnostic consultant at Edison, which offered me opportunities to visit Geneva, offer her support, and discuss the program with faculty. The faculty accepted the classroom and its teacher as a vital part of the building as slowly as parents accepted the notion of a public school preschool. In retrospect, I realize that beginning a program with a strong emphasis on staff awareness is critical if the new program is to become quickly integrated into the school.

An early ally was Sharon Vaughn, the kindergarten teacher. She quickly recognized the importance of preschool education and expressed a deep interest in the curriculum. At this time, although the school district viewed kindergarten as a necessary part of the educational program, few were knowledgeable about appropriate curriculum; consequently, early childhood educators were not specifically chosen to teach kindergarten. Instead, selection was based upon teacher *willingness* to teach at this level.

No training or theoretical base was outlined for the kindergarten program except a "curriculum guide" that was a collection of ideas, units, and suggestions. The district purchased basal reading materials at the "readiness" level that teachers were expected to have their classes complete. A mixture of large- and small-group instruction followed the basal series. Children completed worksheets and workbooks related to skills introduced in the classroom.

Sharon's training, however, included a developmental perspective. I talked with her about the plan-do-review process that is a part of the High/Scope curriculum. (It is not a required part of a developmentally appropriate philosophy, although child choice and children's increasing responsibility for self-management *is*.) She already valued choosing activities and materials that are of interest to five-year-olds, and began arranging her room and daily schedule to allow time for choices, even though she expressed her doubts about the efficiency of letting children choose when there were a large number of students (24 to 25) and only one adult.

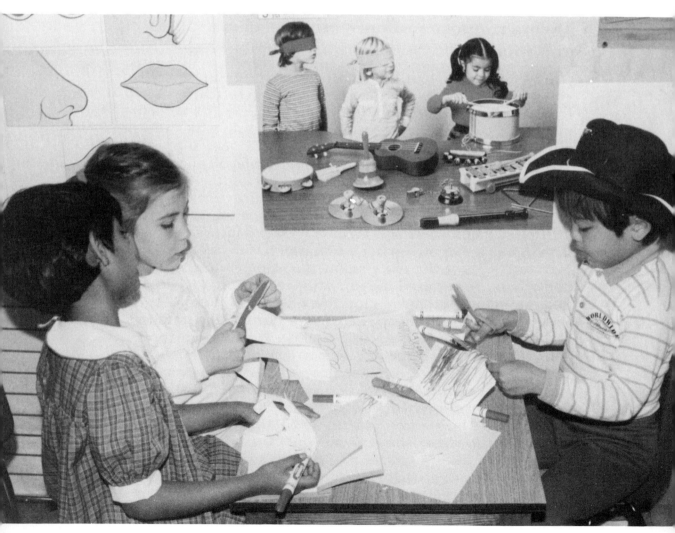

I did not have the answers she sought, but I knew that her classroom frequently promoted the developmental philosophy I was coming to know and accept. I knew, too, that this teacher and this classroom had the potential for facilitating consistent coordination of education for preschoolers and kindergartners. Sharon's knowledge of child development and her intuitive understanding of what we now call developmentally appropriate practice led to the marriage of the preschool and kindergarten programs at Edison, creating a strong unit that could support the early childhood initiatives that were to follow.

Continuing to study all aspects of developmentally appropriate practice

My own thinking during this period and the next two to three years was influenced by study of early childhood practices in the professional literature and some university coursework related to parent involvement. I tried to read every available journal article on topics ranging from literacy to management strategies for preschool and kindergarten classrooms.

Getting support from a network of knowledgeable educators

The network of trainers implementing the High/Scope curriculum across the state was a frequent support system as I struggled to overcome obstacles to implementation. I also received support through my interactions at DESE's annual Conference on the Young Years, which is attended by early childhood educators from public and private settings. These interactions were extremely valuable to me as a kind of sounding board for ideas and problems related to implementation.

Professional meetings also allowed me to hear presentations by nationally recognized professionals in early childhood. Through these presentations I realized the scope and impact of early childhood education and felt a confirmation for developmentally appropriate practices and programs. The presentations also provided intellectual stimulation that spurred me to continue reading about developmental theory and to share what I learned with Geneva, Sharon, and other colleagues in St. Joseph.

Summarizing some of my major "early learnings"

During this period I learned the importance of locating quality personnel who possess a disposition for learning and a willingness to take risks. Geneva and Sharon are important people to me because both women, although different in personality and training, exemplify the qualities needed in early childhood education. They are caring, compassionate, and supportive. They can organize a child-oriented environment. They can live with ambiguity and make decisions. They are themselves learners. Certainly not all early childhood teachers will be clones of a "perfect" model, but the disposition to learn and take risks is essential.

I also learned the importance of developing relationships of mutual trust and respect. From the beginning, I worked to establish relationships with the teachers who would implement the program and those who would extend and support it. I treated them with the kind of trust and respect that I expected them to use with children and with other adults.

Top-down management is not called for in this approach. What is needed, instead, is a trusting relationship in which problems are solved together and decisions are considered from a variety of perspectives.

In addition, staff awareness is essential so that the entire school knows how to support the efforts of the early childhood teacher. Now, as the school's principal, I frequently talk about the early childhood programs, share stories, and include preschool and kindergarten in all schedules. I expect everyone on the staff to consider the early childhood programs as vital and necessary components. It is an expectation backed up with knowledge about what the programs accomplish, their problems, and their visions.

This accomplishment requires developing one's own knowledge base and then sharing it. From the very beginning, I shared whatever I could with Geneva and anyone else who would listen, which expanded their abilities to create appropriate early childhood classrooms. Importantly, my own active involvement as a learner and a risk taker enabled me to serve as a model and to remain enthusiastic.

As a Training of Trainers project participant, I have helped teach summer Institutes that inform preschool and extended day kindergarten teachers about appropriate practices. These week-long Institutes delve intensively into theory and practice, but experience has taught me that this is only a beginning. Ongoing training at the site to extend the experiences of focused training sessions is an essential element of staff development.

Taking the helm

I was appointed principal of Edison School in 1984. I came to this position full of hope, with visions of putting into practice my beliefs about appropriate curriculum, especially providing choices for problem solving, active learning, and thinking and reasoning skills. I quickly faced the challenge of practicing what I believed in the real world of elementary school, from preschool through grade six.

Enrollment at Edison consists of approximately 450 students, and there are 26 full-time staff members. Over 60% of the families show sufficient economic need to qualify for federal free or reduced lunch programs. Those not qualifying are largely from working middle-class homes in a historic neighborhood from the turn of the century and single-family dwellings. Forty percent of the school population is minority, primarily Black. The 60-year-old facility is in excellent condition, and the staff are well-trained veterans of Chapter 1 schools.

Working within a whole-school context

My first year as principal at Edison was a time of learning the role of the principal and establishing a safe school climate. It was a hiatus from concentration on early childhood education and special education as I struggled to manage a school and provide a small measure of instructional leadership.

The preschool and kindergarten programs that I longed to supervise were given only cursory attention. I realized then how difficult it was for administrators to give intensive time to programs in which they have only minimal investment or interest. It was a valuable lesson that taught me to appreciate all the roles a building administrator plays and the difficulty of concentrating effort and maintaining balance within an elementary school.

I continued to attend early childhood conferences and was able to include Geneva and Sharon. Because of increased enrollment, a second kindergarten teacher joined the staff to teach half-day. Orienting another teacher to developmentally appropriate practices was difficult. I began to appreciate more and more the need for solid university training in child development and hiring practices that value the special skills of early childhood teachers.

Applying aspects of a developmentally appropriate philosophy schoolwide

About this time, I was confronting extreme behavior problems with students and learned about and implemented a schoolwide discipline plan that included heavy emphasis on reward and punishment. Although I valued thinking, reasoning, and decision making, I thought that self-discipline and self-regulation would be fostered by this approach.

The kindergarten staff, however, quickly modified the plan. Because I especially valued problem solving in the early years, I accepted their less structured version of the schoolwide plan, somehow thinking that the kindergarten experience was different. A painful experience later taught me that what is appropriate for kindergarten children in terms of sociomoral development is appropriate for children throughout the school, and that practices appropriate to early childhood education cannot be reasonably separated from other levels of schooling. The experience also provoked greater consistency in my thinking and furthered my departure from my behavioristic beginnings.

The critical incident occurred when a two-day in-service was scheduled for all teachers in grades four, five, and six. Nine intermediate teachers at Edison were provided substitutes. I anticipated that student management would be a concern and tried to prepare by making sure that lessons were fully planned. I also wrote notes to the substitutes suggesting reward systems to manage behavior. Because the school had been using a systematic approach and behavioral improvements had occurred, I was hoping that there would be only minor difficulties.

What I didn't expect was my worst fears being realized within minutes of the opening bell. Students quickly discovered that not only did they have a substitute teacher, but so did all the classrooms on the third floor. Misbehavior of every kind took place! I spent two days doing everything possible to maintain safety and control.

As a result of this experience, I came to understand that simply controlling behavior is not sufficient. By relying upon reward and punishment, I was being fooled into thinking that students were developing self-regulation when, in fact, they were merely behaving appropriately when supervised by trusted adults. Had I known then about Piaget's thinking on sociomoral development and the consequences of heteronomy, I would not have been as shocked. This experience prompted me to find ways to promote sociomoral development and problem solving, and early childhood principles and practices became the foundation for my effort.

During my first year as a principal, I learned that I couldn't be all things to all people. I learned that the time invested in early childhood programs was worth it—even when other matters were seemingly more pressing.

I had to learn to trust teachers to take the information I gave them and to experiment with it. My interactions with teachers became conversations focused on feedback about how those experiments were going. According to the teachers, this kind of trust and interaction has been critical.

I also concluded that early childhood practices are definitely not limited to, or only appropriate for, the very young. Problem-solving approaches, a philosophy of active learning, and developmentally appropriate materials and activities have become the foundation for work throughout the school because they make sense for ALL the children. The early childhood classrooms became catalysts for school-wide change.

Widening horizons

During the 1985–86 school year, Edison teachers and I developed a schoolwide goal related to the integration of language arts in the curriculum. We experimented with whole-language strategies and focused attention on the writing process. The kindergarten classrooms began putting less emphasis on completing workbooks and more emphasis on reading aloud and spending time in areas of interest. Sharon Vaughn began incorporating discovery methods with math instruction. She also experimented with ways to have children make plans for their work in various areas and to evaluate their experiences.

Moving toward developmentally appropriate practice in our school

Over the next two years a gradual change occurred. There was a decreasing emphasis on directed teaching, accompanied by an increasing emphasis on discovery and choice. Throughout this period, I gave teachers articles to read related to whole language and active learning. In-service at the building level was designed to strengthen the teachers' knowledge base for theory and practice. An atmosphere that encouraged risk was promoted among students and teachers. I encouraged teachers to experiment. I advocated "trying things out" and said that our mistakes would be constructive errors.

All this occurred while we were still trying to maintain the requirements of the school district in terms of text usage and reading instruction, which were heavily influenced by standard basal pedagogy. It was confusing for me, and I know it was confusing for teachers. On one hand, I promoted basal instruction with groupings and directed teaching; on the other hand, I encouraged experimentation with holistic strategies, risk taking, problem solving, and literature-based instruction.

There were times when teachers didn't want to use workbooks and skills tests, but were afraid not to. Some wanted to experiment with literature sets. I agreed and encouraged them, but always with a nagging guilt that somehow I was not adhering to policy. It was risk taking for grown-ups, and there were times when it was almost frightening.

The results, however, were wonderful! Teachers became enthusiastic about instruction in a way I had never seen before. Children in kindergarten and first grade began to write whole sentences and stories. Literature was important and interesting. Learning to read wasn't just a skill—it was a joy! Seeing the results in terms of attitudes toward learning was the motivation I needed in order to press on.

Moving toward developmentally appropriate practice in our state—Introducing constructivism

During this time, the Director of Early Childhood Education for DESE invited me to join a group of early childhood professionals across the state to develop statewide goals for young children from preschool through grade one. In addition to curriculum, an assessment component was also to be developed. This vision for Missouri's children is now called "Project Construct," and its implementation at Edison has changed the design of our thinking and practice.

The Conference on the Young Years in March 1988 focused on Project Construct. I took with me the Edison early childhood teachers, including grade one, as well as teachers from other district preschools and kindergartens. They were together for the first time as an early childhood team.

There was an electricity about that conference because it was apparent that these ideas called *constructivism* were so very consistent with what we already believed about how children learn, yet they extended far beyond our current level of thinking. First grade teachers had not been heavily involved before this time, and they later revealed that what they heard was more than they could adequately comprehend. This was especially true of group games, which were discussed by the featured speaker Rheta DeVries; they could not understand the significance of games as "real" instruction. They were more comfortable with presentations on emerging literacy because of prior study in this area. The discussions on autonomy were not clear either. There was a sense, however, that this was information of tremendous importance if it could just be understood and applied in a practical way.

In the summer of 1988, I joined 15 other early childhood professionals from Missouri who were participants in Project Construct for a week-long training session with Connie Kamii at the University of Alabama at Birmingham. We each received a set of books related to constructivism and Piagetian theory. I devoured those books after spending an incredible week of intense discussion and training in Birmingham. Although I was a skeptic in terms of putting theory into practice, my theoretical framework provided a basis from which to make decisons. I returned to St. Joseph with new-found confidence and a fund of ideas.

Moving further toward developmentally appropriate practice by bringing "home" what we learned

I met with the Edison early childhood teachers before school began. I provided them with some of the books I had read, especially ones related to group games and logical-mathematical knowledge. Articles on autonomy were shared and discussed. Sharon Azelton, an extended-day kindergarten teacher, and Ronda Chesney, a first grade teacher, had attended an extensive workshop on Success in Reading and Writing, a nonbasal reading approach. They met with me to share what they had learned, and I agreed to proceed with this approach for the coming year. I made clear my own belief, though, that this program was a bridge from reliance on basal manuals and techniques to whole-language instruction.

These meetings were exciting beyond belief. Teachers could hardly wait to share what they were learning, yet there was considerable anxiety as we discussed putting aside basal texts and workbooks. Without question, this was one of the most powerful times for the Edison teachers and for me.

At the same time, Edison School became a pilot site for Project Construct, which meant that the district gave approval for the early childhood programs at Edison to try out the Construct goals and give input to DESE on their use. Being a pilot site relieved some of the pressure to continue implementing all of the district curriculum strategies, such as basal instruction.

My responsibility was to see that quality instruction continued to happen in an atmosphere of "experimentation." I had to assure other administrators that the strategies being used would indeed be effective, assure teachers that risk taking was essential, reassure colleagues that Edison was not going off the deep end, and—in the middle of the night—assure myself that somehow this would all come together as appropriate practice.

Changes in teachers were dramatic as they learned strategies for whole-group instruction. Risk taking became standard practice. Kindergarten and first grade teachers began using the Success program. I read the manuals carefully and tried to give feedback as I observed in classrooms. The teachers, in turn, shared their Success program experiences with other teachers. Amy Schilter, a first grade teacher, became a master at charts. Patti Burri, a first grade teacher for 15 years, was enthralled with the process of group games. Teachers read, discussed, attended Project Construct training sessions, and functioned as a team.

Kindergarten—full-day and half-day—was a central focus. The preschool program continued with its emphasis on thinking and reasoning, which led into a kindergarten where children were given increasing amounts of choice. Problem solving, extended questioning, and active learning were now a regular part of the kindergarten day. First graders continued those strategies from kindergarten. The old "get ready for the next grade" routine quietly disappeared as teachers planned, worked, and studied together across grade levels.

And still more training!—in constructivism

In the summer of 1989, Edison teachers and I attended a week-long training session with participants from other Project Construct sites. Rheta DeVries returned to Missouri to conduct the training. This time we were ready.

This experience pulled together theory and practice. Because the teachers and I had had opportunities to study and teach prior to the training, we were prepared to ask questions and consider theoretical constructs in a way that would not have been possible before.

This week was a turning point for teachers because they consolidated their confidence in their ability to understand child development theory. They gained insight into how to put their understandings into practice. For me, the week provided an opportunity to be both a learner and a leader—a critical combination for building mutual trust and respect.

Building constructivist teachers

Upon our return, we learned that a $20,000 incentive grant written by the early childhood teachers had been approved. The grant would help to improve literacy at Edison by using the Project Construct learning goals and literature-based reading instruction. Edison continued as a pilot site, with new emphasis on assessment. In addition, a new language arts supervisor joined the district, and an integrated language arts approach was introduced districtwide. Edison teachers now confidently set aside workbooks in favor of whole group strategies and active learning.

Both kindergartens expanded their use of interest areas. First grades allotted large blocks of time for recreational reading. The grant funded literature choices and computers for writing and publishing. A parent involvement component was initiated—extending the foundations laid in preschool—so that parents could be informed about the practices of the classroom and encouraged to be actively involved. Mathematics was taught through group games and daily living experiences.

Heavy emphasis was given to sociomoral development, always a concern at Edison. The entire faculty attended an in-service on problem solving and conflict resolution consistent with the theories applied in the early childhood classrooms. In the principal's office, I practiced the process of resolving conflicts by discussion and perspective taking.

Some teachers were reluctant to accept the change from reward and punishment to a problem-solving approach. Many felt pressure from faculty to use the old ways. I couldn't blame them when I remembered my own skepticism, but I was determined to practice what I believed. I found promoting sociomoral development to be exhausting, especially on a schoolwide basis, and there were setbacks, such as situations when I "ran out of time" and resorted to efficient methods of handing out punishment, but the results justified the additional effort.

During this time I realized that the role of principal as risk taker included acting as a protective buffer for teachers in dealing with the central office's concerns about appropriate curriculum. I provided the defense for our departure from standard practices such as basals and worksheets. I took the risk of supporting teaching methods I had not actually tried and sold those methods to others as effective practice, freeing teachers to be risk takers in their classrooms. Risk taking for me involved faith in a solid framework of theory plus confidence in my ability to encourage and communicate with teachers in a way that would help them understand not only what to do but why.

I have developed a presentation entitled "Building Constructivist Teachers." It emphasizes the importance of

1. forming a trusting relationship with staff, and

2. sharing knowledge of appropriate theory and its implications for practice.

Over the years I have consistently shared articles, books, and my own observations with any teacher who would listen. I have focused my daily interactions on curriculum and instruction and tried to point out every possible way improvements could be made that would be more consistent with theory.

Hanging in there

I think teachers trust me because I listen to their point of view and try very hard to see things from their perspective. I respect them tremendously, and they, in turn, respect my knowledge of curriculum and my persistence, even when confronting problems.

Pressure from other administrators and teachers is a problem because there are no quick answers. Developmentally appropriate practice is *not* a quick fix for every problem. Unfortunately, when using unfamiliar methods, a certain amount of pressure to defend those methods is felt. I felt pressure to produce and to be accountable. There is much less pressure now, however, because the more I know about theory and the more I practice what I know, the more confident I am about my ability to explain why Edison teachers use certain methods or materials instead of others.

I believe it *critical* that principals who want to develop appropriate early childhood classrooms first develop in themselves a knowledge base that will create the confidence necessary to withstand outside pressures. I've also learned that you don't have to know it all before getting started; you do, however, have to be willing to take risks and to be imperfect.

I attribute a large measure of my success to "hanging in there." After I studied the theory and gained increasing confidence that what I was trying to accomplish was indeed theoretically sound and not just another bandwagon program, I persevered . . . and still do. When discouraged, I talked with my network of colleagues across the state, or read more or talked more with teachers. I haven't given up on what I think is appropriate practice, and the result of that perseverance is ongoing growth and success.

Today and beyond

Today, Edison students, especially those who have been involved in the early childhood change process, are able to solve some problems by talking with each other and considering another person's point of view. They see reading and writing as meaningful activities. They can explain the answers they get in mathematical problems and look for ways to apply what they know.

Edison early childhood teachers have a knowledge base from which they make decisions about appropriate activities in their classrooms. They are able to plan instruction that is meaningful based upon their observations of children.

Teachers are confident in their ability to solve problems with children and can readily use a variety of strategies that promote sociomoral development. The teachers and I are less dependent upon each other's support and encouragement and are beginning to pursue our individual interests.

Teachers function as a team, relying upon one another for support, encouragement, and insight. All the early childhood teachers have made presentations to other teachers and have experienced visits from professionals outside the school and outside the district. When talking with others, they are able to explain not only what they are doing but why.

My role as a leader has also evolved. I still observe and give feedback and offer food for thought in terms of things to read and think about. I still give encouragement when problems occur and act as a sounding board; however, at this point, I am much more a facilitator than a leader for the group. Sometimes I think the teachers don't "need" me. When this happens, I remind myself that this was the ultimate goal. I wanted change to occur in such a way that it was believed as well as practiced. Truly, this has happened at Edison.

Developmentally appropriate practices are established in the minds of our teachers. Policy and administrative staff could try to suppress it, but it is here to stay. I came to the principalship eager to make a difference, and early childhood education gave me my opportunity.

Way to go

Along the way there were certainly problems, some of which still exist. There is a lack of adequate funds to purchase materials to begin new programs and a lack of control at the building level over the dollars spent for instructional equipment and materials. The whole issue of assessment and high-stakes testing remains despite our efforts to develop assessment strategies consistent with the goals for early childhood education. There are also the children and families who come to school with a wide diversity of backgrounds and beliefs.

The constant challenge persists of explaining to administrators, teachers, parents, and the community the value of appropriate practices for young children. For some, the value of early childhood education itself must be defended. These are those who believe that the purpose of early childhood education is getting children ready for formal schooling. There individuals fail to see the importance of approaching education as a developmental process. The challenge is to communicate what *is* appropriate and *why* it makes sense to think about learning as a constructive process. Obviously, challenges remain. We still have a way to go.

I continue to promote risk taking and a climate for growth. I talk with teachers a lot. I read, I listen, and I observe. I certainly didn't know all I need to know when I began, and I don't know everything I need to know now. I do know, though, that I can find or figure out what to do by reading, thinking, listening, and talking to others. The teachers, in particular, are a tremendous resource.

I've built a team by caring about individuals, respecting each teacher's level of development, and setting expectations for the group as a whole. My own knowledge of early childhood practices has given me credibility at home and across the state. My personal and professional relationships with teachers have made what I know grow into a thriving example of appropriate practices at work.

"Coming to know" has been the most exciting professional experience of my life. The best part is that the knowing never ends, and the lives of young children—as well as their teachers—are better because of it.

Postscript . . . one year later

"Coming to know" is a developmental process, and I have now moved into a new stage of my own professional development. In August 1991, I was selected to be the Language Arts Supervisor for grades K–12 for the St. Joseph Public Schools. I approach this new position with enthusiasm for the opportunity to make a difference in the lives of others through language arts curriculum and instruction with a broader view than just a single building. With a heavy heart, though, I leave Edison School and the elementary principalship.

As I now reflect on the total experience of Edison School, I realize that one of my goals all along was to inspire in others the confidence and conviction to be decision makers and risk takers. I have given seven years of my professional life to this endeavor, with the hope that early childhood teachers at Edison would grow and learn in ways beyond my influence. Now that I will no longer be the principal at Edison, the teachers there will have this special opportunity to stretch their own abilities and knowledge of appropriate practice. As Language Arts Supervisor, I will, of course, be available to them for consultation and support. In turn, they will be available to me as a sounding board for ideas concerning implementation in other buildings. As a result, new doors of opportunity are opening for all of us.

Suggested reading for principals

Bird, L. B. (1989). *Becoming a whole language school: The Fair Oaks story.* Katonah, NY: Richard C. Owen Publishers.

DeVries, R., with Kohlberg, L. (1990). *Programs of early education: The constructivist view.* Washington, DC: National Association for the Education of Young Children. (Original work published 1987 by Longman)

Duckworth, E. (1987). *The having of wonderful ideas and other essays.* New York: Teachers College Press.

Goodman, K. (1986). *What's whole in whole language?* Portsmouth, NH: Heinemann Educational Books, Inc.

National Association of Elementary School Principals. (1990). *Early childhood education and the elementary school principal.* Alexandria, VA: Author.

National Association of State Boards of Education. (1988). *Right from the start.* Alexandria, VA: Author.

CHAPTER

Developing Appropriate Practices in the Kindergarten: A District-Level Perspective

Larry May

My story of implementing developmentally appropriate practices in the public school setting is still being written. The story's plot has evolved through 23 years in a variety of jobs in the field of education: elementary teacher; secondary teacher; elementary principal; junior high principal; senior high principal; and, most recently, Assistant Superintendent of Curriculum and Instruction in the Turner Unified Schools in Kansas City, Kansas.

The breadth of this experience has perhaps afforded me an opportunity to see the K–12 public school program differently from those with more limited experience. Although I thoroughly enjoy working with children and teachers at all grade levels, I find something special about young children and their teachers.

My approach to schooling

My philosophical understanding of the learning process has developed with the accumulation of my professional experiences. Kohlberg and Mayer (1972) outlined three streams of educational thought: romanticism, cultural transmission, and the cognitive developmental or interactional approach. Romanticism presents the purpose of schooling to provide nourishment that triggers the unfolding of innate, prepatterned, predetermined stages in children's development. In this view, social, emotional, and physical development are viewed as biological processes independent of cognitive growth.

The cultural transmission view emphasizes that the environment must input knowledge into the child, who is likened to an empty vessel or a blank slate. This is the world of the behaviorist and programmed learning. This view has been the predominant view for the past 30 years or more and served the American industrial society very well; unfortunately, it has led to many of the inappropriate practices that have sprung up in kindergarten classrooms all over the country.

The third view is the cognitive developmental approach, which holds that knowledge must be "constructed" by the child through an interaction or dialogue with the physical and social environment. This is the philosophy I believe is required of an "information society" such as ours.

My own schooling in the cultural transmission model influenced my initial teaching philosophy. Later, when I grappled with issues and concerns as an elementary principal, my thinking shifted to more of a romantic view. I became dissatisfied with the narrow emphasis on skills, and it was easy to believe that if we just trusted children to learn, they would learn what they needed to know.

My study of, and involvement in, the early childhood education movement over the past eight years, however, led me to seek a more adequate explanation of learning and development. I became disenchanted with the romantic view of a child's education as I came to realize that "trusting the child to do the right thing" was inadequate to the challenges of education. As my understanding of the cognitive developmental approach has grown, I have found it to provide a better explanation of learning and development. My commitment to the cognitive developmental approach reflects my current belief that learners, regardless of their age, "construct" meaning from their experiences.

If we are to assist in the process of helping schools understand learning as constructive, however, we must also know how to influence the change process. Unfortunately, schools seldom welcome change. Too often, they seem to view change as an unpleasant intruder. As a result, I have become a student not only of early childhood education but also of the change process for individuals and organizations.

Facilitating change: Four cornerstones upon which to build

When I began my administrative career 20 years ago, I wanted to develop a school in which people didn't complain. The only way I knew how to do this was by involving people in the decision-making process in order to create ownership of the decisions. I knew that when teachers developed ownership for an idea, the idea usually worked.

My administrative philosophy still embraces ownership as a key element, but it has grown to include three other elements or cornerstones: vision, support, and capacity. I've come to believe that all four cornerstones must receive adequate attention in order to ensure the successful implementation of any idea in public schools; therefore, when seeking to implement appropriate practices in our kindergarten program, I reflected upon these four cornerstones.

I envision change similar to constructing a building. If that building is to be long lasting, it must be built upon a solid foundation. The foundation must be carefully planned and deliberately built upon these four cornerstones before work on the building can commence. Whenever I want to create, enhance, or implement a program or a concept, I first look at the foundation, analyze the current strengths and weaknesses of the foundation, and set about to strengthen the four cornerstones.

The four cornerstones are both independent and interdependent. All must receive adequate attention, and as one stone is made stronger, that strength has a positive impact on the other cornerstones. As the vision becomes clearer and more focused, for example, teachers, principals, and others who are involved in the change process begin to understand the

individual and organizational capacities that need to be enhanced and the type and amount of support needed. If involved in developing the vision and the program, these individuals are more likely to acquire a sense of ownership.

Likewise, when an organization increases support for a project, more people can receive training, which, in turn, enhances both their capacity and opportunity for forging a clearer vision; and when people understand a project better, they are able to assume more leadership. These understandings of the change process, in conjunction with a constructivist approach to schooling, framed my efforts to implement developmentally appropriate practice in Turner's early childhood programs (which included two full-day early childhood special-education classrooms, two transitional first grades, two extended-day kindergarten classrooms, and eight half-day kindergarten classrooms).

The Turner Project

In my previous position as an elementary school principal in an overseas American school, I had the opportunity to develop and implement an early childhood education program for 200 students ages three to six. Because of that experience and my interest in early childhood education, one of the first tasks I initiated as assistant superintendent of the Turner Unified Schools was a meeting with the 14 early childhood teachers and 5 elementary principals.

In the beginning

My purpose for that initial meeting was to determine the type of kindergarten program currently in existence, as well as to assess the staff's satisfaction with the existing program. Dissatisfaction surfaced very quickly, especially around two topics:

1. measuring academic performance of students via a standardized achievement test; and

2. the district's heavy emphasis on basal programs and their accompanying worksheets/ditto sheets.

The Turner School District is a suburban/rural, primarily blue-collar community, with a high incidence of children from low-income families. The district was operating from a typical cultural transmission philosophy. The job of kindergarten teachers was to ensure that students got the "right information" so they would fit into the first grade program. Many teachers talked about their frustration—and the frustration of their students—in coping with these two disturbing elements of the instructional program.

Teachers were clearly unhappy with the current direction and vision of the kindergarten program. They believed that the district's curriculum supported and reinforced inappropriate practices because of its emphasis on testing and paper-and-pencil activities. Teachers did not express ownership in the existing program. They also believed that they lacked the capacity and the permission to make changes.

Although many of the 14 teachers were unhappy with the program, they had been following it for so many years that they did not know any other way, nor even how to question current practices. We discussed setting up a multiyear process to analyze the situation, study the alternatives, and develop a new program.

I knew that the teachers needed to create a sense of ownership in the change process as well as in the revised program. They had to be involved in the formulation of a new vision for the program. Only then would they be able to determine the individual and organizational capacities needed—and the type and amount of organizational support required—to make the endeavor a success.

I also knew from my previous experiences that the selection of an outside third party would be critical to our efforts. We decided to investigate several area colleges and universities to see if we could find a good match for the Turner Project. I used this situation to create ownership in the process. I arranged for all the early childhood teachers to visit the institutions and the university personnel involved. Obviously, the university and the facilitator would play a major role in the direction our vision would take.

Creating time to study, to discuss, and to collectively construct the vision and develop capacities to implement developmentally appropriate practices in classrooms is a crucial support issue. We developed a plan to cancel one morning section of kindergarten and one afternoon section each month. This provided teachers with two 3-hour blocks of time each month. Half-day substitutes were provided for teachers who taught in full-day programs.

I explained the plan to the board of education, presented how I would use my budget for the project, and easily gained their approval. This was not an issue or a project that they found controversial.

The district's superintendent similarly granted approval. Early childhood education had not been of special interest to either the school board or the school superintendent, but they also gave me complete freedom to develop and implement the program.

Implementing the project

Once the organization's support was in place, I confronted the issue of enhancing our capacities as educators to work with young children in more appropriate ways. Could teachers improve in this area? Could they begin to see the different philosophical approaches and the influence that each of those approaches has on classroom practice? Could they develop the capacity to design and implement appropriate practices in their classrooms? Could they, through this process, acquire the ownership and the commitment for maintaining such a program? Could they demonstrate support for each other as they wrestled to construct their own knowledge of appropriate early childhood practices? Could they spread the vision and acquire the support of their principals and fellow teachers in making significant modifications to the program? Thus, we embarked on a quest to answer these questions.

The bimonthly seminars with the university facilitator and the teachers began in the fall of 1988. The facilitator developed a format of readings, discussions, reflections, journal maintenance, and classroom visitations. Many teachers quickly discovered that mere dissatisfaction with the status quo did not provide them with the knowledge and insights to develop a new program.

Managing the article readings, the journal, and discussions with the other teachers was not easy; it was demanding; it was time consuming; and, at times, it was uncomfortable because the process questioned many current practices. During the two years of the Turner Project, however, teachers became less reliant upon textbooks and worksheets and more involved in designing their classroom curriculums.

I think the seminars were the key to the project's success. Through the information provided by the facilitator, teachers grappled with ideas and concepts. Articles were shared to stimulate teachers' thinking processes. Teachers were challenged to begin the process of constructing and defending their new understandings of the developmental nature of childhood and the way in which children construct their knowledge and understanding of the world around them. The journals provided an opportunity for private dialogue with the facilitator. As the teachers experimented in their classrooms, they also shared their successes and insights with each other.

Several teachers took advantage of the opportunity to earn graduate credit through independent study with the university facilitator. Nearly all the participating teachers attended external workshops, seminars, and/or conferences throughout the year. A team of four teachers developed and presented a program on the project, in conjunction with the facilitator, at both a state-level and a national meeting of the National Association for the Education of Young Children. I took every opportunity I could to support their professional growth, including making time and money available for conferences and workshops.

Assessing the project's success

Have all teachers designed and implemented totally appropriate learning environments for their students? No. Have all teachers modified their programs *to some extent* along a continuum leading toward appropriate practices? Yes.

The overreliance on the basal reading programs and on paper-and-pencil and workbook ditto sheets has significantly declined. The practice of standardized achievement testing for kindergarten students has been discontinued.

As expected, some teachers made remarkable changes in their classrooms, while others made less noticeable change; nevertheless, change has become integrated into the Turner schools. Our district statement, "Turner Schools—Our Business Is Learning," has taken on an expanded meaning to include the emphasis that we, as educators, are also in the business of learning our profession. Obviously, schools in which teachers are alive and learning and constructing their own understandings of appropriate practices will be better learning environments for children.

The Turner Project also had a major impact on our elementary program. As the teachers, the facilitator, and I struggled with the question of spreading appropriate practices to first grade and beyond, the whole-language movement was recognized as an excellent vehicle to promote

appropriate practices throughout the elementary grades. The emphasis of the whole-language approach was consistent with the teaching emphasis early childhood teachers were beginning to use: building upon what students already know; learning in a meaningful context; progressing from the whole to the part; teaching skills within a larger context; involving students in an active social learning process; and, of course, use of good children's literature. Furthermore, a number of our elementary teachers were already experimenting with whole-language concepts.

It became clear to me that this was the most convenient and practical way to help elementary teachers understand the shift in thinking that was occurring within our early childhood staff. Many of our early childhood teachers became resources for other grade-level teachers as they began the process of implementing the whole-language concept. Appropriate practices are appropriate practices, regardless of the age of the child. I was very excited about the level of commitment to change and growth exhibited within our elementary teaching staff.

Project shortcomings

I am critical of my efforts in two areas:

1. A major disappointment is my failure with the five elementary principals. As an elementary principal myself, I had found it easy to create ownership through a shared vision and common goals, to provide the necessary psychological and material supports, and to enhance the capabilities of teachers; I assumed the same would be true for these principals. Consequently, I underestimated the principals' lack of understanding of developmentally appropriate practices and of the change process itself. I did not develop for principals the kinds of opportunities to develop ownership that were provided for their teachers. I "invited" their active participation, but did not have a backup plan when my invitation failed to create the necessary involvement.

Instead, I assumed the responsibility for providing the resources of time, money, and direction. I realize now that I deprived principals of an opportunity to acquire ownership in the Turner Project. Few principals attended the seminars, which were held in each of the elementary schools. As a result, they did not grow along with their teachers in understanding appropriate practices or the cognitive developmental approach.

Principals assumed the stance of passive supporters. I guess they figured that if I was willing to assume responsibility for the program, they would let me do it! (Their active involvement took a significant turn toward the positive, however, as more and more of their teachers became involved with the whole-language movement. Several of them became committed to supporting the growth of whole-language practices by their teachers.)

During the 1990–91 school year, I took steps to correct this mistake. The facilitator (whose involvement with the district was renewed) and I tried to meet with principals on a monthly basis to discuss their concerns and to jointly develop strategies for encouraging and supporting developmentally appropriate practices in *all* their classrooms, from kindergarten through sixth grade. I shared my disappointment with them as well as my commitment to improve the process during the coming year. I hoped that they were more willing to assume instructional leadership in this area.

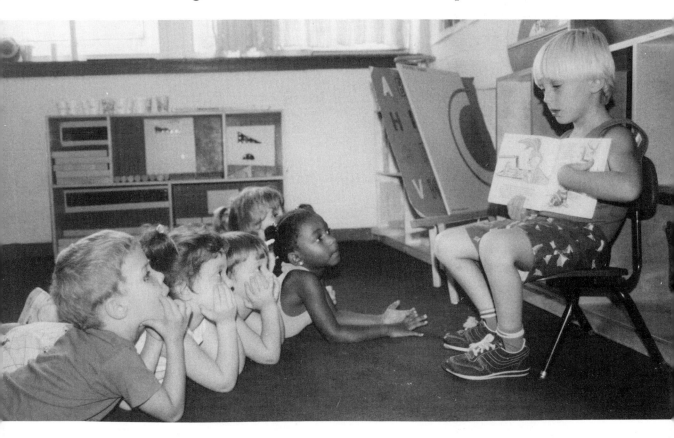

2. The minor disappointment was the failure to involve parents to a higher degree. Our parents did not oppose the project; they were simply uninformed. Several of the teachers did an excellent job of involving parents and keeping them informed, but that was due to their own strengths and orientation.

Our failure to adequately explain developmentally appropriate practices to parents is illustrated by a parent's comment to her child's kindergarten teacher at the end of the school year. After telling the teacher how much her child loved school and how the child was reading books and environmental print, the parent asked, "Did my child learn anything this year?"

It was my intention in the new school year to keep parents apprised of our efforts to identify kindergarten educational outcomes, revise report cards, and improve parent-teacher conferences. In addition, several teachers were developing a classroom newsletter for parents to better inform them about classroom activities.

The transformation model of change

I have briefly discussed the four cornerstones upon which I believe lasting change must be built. The four cornerstones of vision, ownership, capacity, and support can now be examined in relation to the Turner Project.

Vision

Although the bases are not hierarchial, I see the obvious starting point as vision. Without having a fairly clear idea of where one would like to go, the odds of reaching that objective are greatly diminished. One of the first questions I think administrators must ask themselves is, "What is the purpose— What is the aim of school?" Specifically, what is the purpose of our early childhood programs? What is our philosophy?

The Turner mission statement is, "Turner Schools—Our Business Is Learning." We believe that we are in the business of helping children learn, as well as being in a business that is learning. Increasingly, learning implies the active construction of knowledge and understandings related to that knowledge. It is not simply the acquisition of skills or pieces of information or unrelated facts.

The question, "What is the purpose of schooling," is therefore critical, because inappropriate as well as appropriate practices reflect the philosophical approach that is employed in the classroom. What do we believe about how five-year-old children learn?

Organizations such as the National Association for the Education of Young Children (NAEYC) (Bredekamp, 1987), the National Association of Elementary School Principals (NAESP, 1990), and the National Association of State Boards of Education (NASBE, 1988) have developed exceptional reports and recommendations around which the Turner District is building its vision statements. Dialogue around such documents is an ideal strategy for school districts to use with teachers, administrators, parents, and board members to develop an appropriate and compelling vision. Another excellent source for developing vision statements is the practical experiences of teachers who are using developmentally appropriate curricular and instructional practices.

The Turner vision, which embraces the cognitive-developmental approach, is congruent with the district's mission statement. Many administrators at both the building and district levels, however, lack sufficient experience and/or training in early childhood education. These individuals must be provided appropriate training to enable them to not only see the vision but fulfill a role as "keeper of the vision."

Vision must be simultaneously loose and tight. On one hand, the district vision must be tight enough that everyone in the organization clearly understands its direction. The vision cannot be so rigid and tightly defined, however, that no one has an opportunity to embellish or personalize the vision. In other words, the vision must clearly indicate that we are all headed in the same direction, while at the same time providing individuals within the organization an opportunity to develop ownership of the vision. The real power of a vision "comes alive" only when it is shared.

The Turner district has a vision of what its teachers can be: active, informed, committed professionals who understand the cognitive and developmental nature of children. These professionals should be committed to their roles as early childhood educators and should accept responsibility for helping parents and other elementary teachers understand how children learn and why teachers organize their classrooms and daily schedules as they do.

The school district has a vision of the role of its principals as key educational leaders in their buildings and at the district level, ready and able to explain our approach to parents, board members, and other district administrators. I see principals as the primary constructors of learning environments in their schools. Principals are the keepers and conveyors of the vision of their developmentally appropriate programs.

Although this role of the principal is part of our vision, it is not yet a reality, as already discussed. One of the major goals as we entered our third year of the project was to assist principals in developing into the type of educational leaders necessary for the continued success and institutionalization of the program.

The advice I would offer to superintendents interested in developing appropriate practices districtwide is to implement strategies involving principals at every step. Many of our teachers responded enthusiastically and energetically to developing appropriate practices but were cautious because of the perceived lack of support and commitment from their principals. Principals must also be helped to understand the benefits of changing their instructional programs toward developmentally appropriate practices and be afforded opportunities to develop the necessary leadership skills.

Ownership

I believe that most of the past failures of educational innovations have been due to the lack of ownership. In order for any new program to become the accepted way of doing business, a high level of ownership must be developed. Teachers have to feel some commitment to, some belief in, some dedication toward, the new program. In order for developmentally appropriate practices to become the norm in all of our classrooms, teachers not only must see the vision and develop needed skills but must come to believe in their hearts that implementing appropriate practices is the best way to help children learn.

As a district, we value teachers as professionals. I realize that our most valuable resource is our professional staff. They are a veritable gold mine of talent, yet I have found that teachers need to be nurtured and supported to the point that they believe themselves to be professionals. Significant, ongoing change happens in classrooms because of teachers, not administrators. Consequently, considerable time and effort need to be invested in this area of ownership. The more creative and successful we are in helping teachers develop ownership, the sooner new programs will be integrated into school districts.

In the Turner Project, teachers were involved from the beginning. Based upon discussions with early childhood teachers, we decided to systematically examine district kindergarten curricular and instructional practices. Our program seemed to be driven by what first grade teachers thought was needed in kindergarten. (In turn, the first grade program was determined by second grade teachers, who, in turn, had their program dictated by third grade teachers, and so on.)

The entire group of 14 teachers visited and interviewed several area universities to determine which program would be best for the Turner schools. After selecting a university and determining the facilitator, teachers played a major role in determining the agendas and schedule for meetings.

It took several meetings before teachers were convinced they needed to actually analyze what they were doing in their classrooms. They kept asking and waiting to be told what to do next, but the facilitator refused to tell them what to do.

If teachers were to develop an understanding of the cognitive nature of learning, they too would have to construct their own knowledge, as opposed to simply being told what to do. The importance of reading the professional literature and entering into a dialogue regarding that literature was strongly encouraged. The process emphasized that they are the professionals in their classrooms who determine the learning environment and curriculum. The facilitator continued to insist that they become informed decision makers.

Capacity

The concept of capacity applies both to the organization and to individuals. An organization, as well as each individual within the organization, needs to develop the capacity to encourage change, to support change, and to see change as a natural and necessary component. The level of organizational health is indicative of a district's ability to handle planned change.

I believe that teachers should know what their profession deems to be sound practice (see, for example, position statements by NAEYC [Bredekamp, 1987] and NAESP

[1990]). They need to develop the skills to implement that knowledge into daily practice in their classrooms and to apply those practices to individual students, as opposed to applying the knowledge to the entire group. I want our teachers to be able to exercise informed judgment.

Incorporating developmentally appropriate practices into classrooms may be a major shift from the way your district is currently doing business. If appropriate practices are not the norm (and they weren't in our district), then teachers must be provided with opportunities to acquire and refine new knowledge, learn necessary skills to implement such practices, and develop the orientations (dispositions) required in order to sucessfully move into the new program.

I have found that a critical step in this area of capacity is the use of an outside resource, an outside expert. This consultant can help plan and present staff development activities and can provide staff with a friendly resource with whom they can consult. This person should serve as a facilitator to the change process, not as a hired gun to enforce the new program. Ownership must be created through the discussions of, and grappling with, developmentally appropriate practices and their implementation into the classroom.

Support

The area of support is where I and other central office administrators live and earn our keep as contributors to the learning process. Although I can and do play a significant role in creating vision, building ownership, and enhancing capacity, my real value is in helping an organization shift gears and in generating support for the shift. Support can come in many forms, including . . .

Philosophy: Central office administrators know and can articulate what they believe. This includes our beliefs about how children learn (for example, the cognitive-developmental philosophy versus other philosophies); our beliefs about who is in charge of classrooms (for example, teachers versus basal programs, the district curriculum, or standardized tests); our beliefs about teachers being involved in decision making at the building level; our beliefs about empowering professional educators through staff development and organizational structures and through support and encouragement for their continual growth as individuals and as members of our organization; our beliefs about the role parents play in their children's education and the way in which we welcome them into our schools; and our beliefs about, and respect for, children and childhood.

Time: Administrators often must be creative in order to find time for group discussions, seminars, and planning. Teachers never have enough time to do all they want to do, let alone extra time for meetings. The school district must support efforts to provide teachers with the necessary time to learn about and implement new ways of doing things.

Personnel: At the district level, we can send very powerful messages about what is important through personnel decisions. Both voluntary and involuntary transfers can be used to support and strengthen the stated vision. Providing additional personnel to support developmentally appropriate practices is a powerful strategy. For the first two years of the project, for example, the Turner District supported five full-day kindergarten/transitional first grade classrooms at an expense to the district of 2.5 FTE staff members. These classrooms permitted more appropriate learning experiences for children identified as at-risk.

Money: Money is a resource, a means to an end—actually a means to a variety of ends. Incorporating developmentally appropriate practices into classrooms is not an expensive endeavor in and of itself. Our principals and teachers discovered that when money was not spent on inappropriate materials such as workbooks, for example, there was more money for appropriate materials.

Training and staff development activities, however, do cost money. If the vision is a district vision, then the district bears some responsibility for providing the necessary resources. As a district, we send clear messages by the types of training and materials provided to teachers. In conjunction with its focus on developmentally appropriate practice, the district has doubled its professional development budget to approximately one percent of its total general fund budget. We have a responsibility to provide appropriate learning environments that are conducive to, and supportive of, appropriate practices.

Policy: Any shift in the way we do business should be supported by appropriate policy and administrative regulation. This ensures that everyone in the organization is aware of the direction being established. It also provides a legal base from which to operate. Several principals began asking for this support, and we began a process of identifying which policies needed to be modified to be more consistent with developmentally appropriate practice.

Power: Power, as defined here, is the potential means of successfully influencing the behavior of others toward the attainment of a specific outcome. Based upon my readings and experiences, I have identified three key sources of power: position power, information power, and personal power. Position power is power invested in an organizational position, for example, a superintendency, a principalship, a kindergarten teaching position. Information power is the knowledge we possess and our ability to apply that knowledge. In an information society such as ours, knowledge is a driving commodity, and it is cheap and available. Personal power includes many qualities, including the ability to develop and maintain rapport, to listen carefully, to communicate, to care, and to have sufficient energy to use the other qualities.

The reason that change that is planned and instigated at the central office level is such a powerful strategy is because the superintendent has the potential to access all levels of power to a greater extent than anyone else in the organization. When superintendents understand the cognitive-developmental philosophy of learning and developmentally appropriate practices; possess interpersonal skills of rapport, listening, and empowerment; have connections with authorities in the area of early childhood education; and bring all of these resources to the district, change seems to magically occur. Of course, it isn't magic at all; it is simply sound planning for, and implementation of, a new way of doing business.

This issue of power is important for anyone interested in influencing the behavior of others, whether they be subordinates, peers, or superiors. Information and personal power are accessible to anyone willing to acquire the necessary knowledge, skills, and orientations. Teachers and parents, as well as administrators, have full access to these power bases, and, effectively used, they can be incredibly potent.

Conclusion

As a profession, we already know what are appropriate and inappropriate practices in early childhood education. As a profession, we already know how to make changes at the district, building, and classroom level. As a profession, therefore, we need to develop the courage and strategies unique to our situation and help to change schools. The strategies outlined here have not been complex or expensive to implement. The Turner Project serves as an example of what can be initiated at the superintendent's level to assist a district in its efforts toward appropriate practices.

As a profession, we have run out of excuses, and we are running out of time. Our children deserve to learn in developmentally appropriate classrooms. The ground has already been broken. We simply need to come to grips with our beliefs and values about children and learning and the purposes of schools, then successfully adapt practices to our particular settings. Although this requires courage, commitment, and leadership, these three qualities are widely distributed within the human resources that our public schools already possess. Our schools, and society at large, can no longer afford to ignore and squander the potential of our children.

Postscript . . . one year later

The more I work the change process within systems, the more I come to understand the "interrelatedness" of everything within the system. A change or shift in one part of the organization affects other parts of the organization, even though it may take a little while for the impact to be felt. As kindergarten programs move toward more appropriate curriculum and instructional practices, first and second grades are affected and, eventually, nearly all grade levels begin to feel the change. If a system is to provide an environment that fosters improvement, it must be ready to deal with change throughout the organization.

Another major learning has been my appreciation of the role played by the system in the change process. For example, school districts often support teachers' professional growth in instructional practices by sending them to workshops, seminars, and training events. Teachers frequently learn new skills and practices and come back enthusiastic about applying their new knowledge to the classroom, but they return to a system that remains as they left it. As a result, teachers have had to try to make significant changes in environments not designed to support those changes.

From a systems viewpoint, teachers have little control over most aspects of the system; rather, the system's leadership has control over factors such as scheduling, resources, assignments, student/teacher ratios, classroom furniture, and so forth. Consequently, I've come to believe that building and district-level administrators are key players in the creation of an environment that supports and sustains significant change over time.

When innovative efforts fail, it is nearly always the result of the system, not the individual attempting the change. Teachers cannot create and sustain significant change without the active support of the administration.

If, therefore, a system is serious about implementing developmentally appropriate practices, it must be willing and able to provide ongoing support structures. Such support structures include professional development activities and opportunities, resources, time, parent information programs, vehicles for informing and involving other staff members throughout the system, policies and administrative regulations supporting the change, and the recognition and celebration of little steps in the right direction.

I will take these insights with me to my new position, which became effective July 1, 1991, as Superintendent of the Southeast Polk Community Schools. I plan to employ a similar process in the district's seven elementary schools, in which some efforts toward developmentally appropriate practices have already been initiated. In the meantime, the Turner Schools are continuing their efforts toward appropriate practices. Through a grant from the State Department, three developmentally appropriate full-day kindergarten programs for at-risk students were implemented in August 1991. One of the kindergarten teachers who participated in the Turner Project has assumed leadership of the new program.

Suggested reading for superintendents

Bennis, W., & Nanus, B. (1985). *Leaders: The strategies for taking charge.* New York: Harper & Row.

DeVries, R., & Kohlberg, L. (1990). *Constructivist early education: Overview and comparison with other programs.* Washington, DC: National Association for the Education of Young Children. (Original work published 1987 by Longman)

Schlechty, P. C. (1990). *Schools for the 21st century.* San Francisco: Jossey-Bass.

Seefeldt, C. (Ed.). (1987). *The early childhood curriculum: A review of current research.* New York: Teachers College Press.

Senge, P. M. (1990). *The fifth discipline.* New York: Doubleday.

References

Bredekamp, S. (Ed.). (1987). *Developmentally appropriate practice in early childhood programs serving children from birth through age 8* (exp. ed.). Washington, DC: National Association for the Education of Young Children.

Kohlberg, L., & Mayer, R. (1972). Development as the aim of education. *Harvard Educational Review, 42*(4), 449–496.

National Association for Elementary School Principals. (1990). *Early childhood education and the elementary school principal: Standards for quality programs for young children.* Alexandria, VA: Author.

National Association of State Boards of Education. (1988). *Right from the start:* Alexandria, VA: Author.

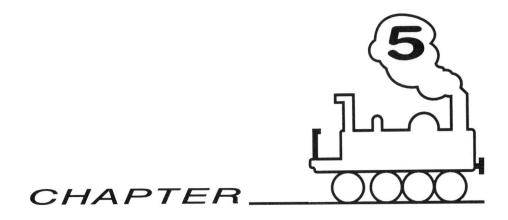

CHAPTER

Parent Power: The Developmental Classroom Project

Linnea Anderson and The Parent Support Group for the Developmental Classroom

In September 1990, as the Developmental Classroom Project began its second year at Baltimore's Garrett Heights Elementary School, there was a sense of cautious optimism among the parents who had worked together thousands of hours to make the Project a reality. Intimate conversations with individual parents might reveal excitement in small doses, but were always tempered with caution.

Much had been invested. Setbacks had been the norm rather than the exception. Adults who perhaps had initially been naive in their idealism were now seasoned fighters—individuals who knew how to fire off letters of protest and knew better than to expect a response. As a small group of parents who began meeting in private homes three years ago with the vague goal of educational reform, we have come a long way, but we also understand the distance yet to go.

We have become activists who understand that change—especially change within a large, bureaucratic institution—

does not happen overnight. Rather, it comes in incremental doses, a victory here and there within a context of wider, systemic problems.

We have also learned that the changes one can make are not predictable. Sometimes they result from difficult, nose-to-nose fights. Sometimes change happens seemingly by accident—positive effects felt from the inexorable shifting of a huge bureaucracy. We are parents who have discovered how to conserve our energies for future battles by carefully picking our fights in the present.

A bit of background

In the fall of 1990, we had a lot to be optimistic about. Garrett Heights Elementary School had seven developmentally appropriate classrooms—the first in the district—ranging from prekindergarten to second grade. There were committed, enthusiastic teachers, three of them new and hand-picked, all poised to teach children in a hands-on, noncompetitive atmosphere. There was also a dynamic and experienced part-time trainer/coordinator, drawn from the ranks of parents, who was helping teachers instruct in a non-teacher-directed environment.

Systemwide, there was a growing perception that Garrett Heights was a school to watch. School administrators called it a model, and there was at least one other city elementary school with a kindergarten class designed from the experience of Garrett Heights. Early childhood curriculum was being rewritten at the district level to reflect a new emphasis on developmentally appropriate practice. In addition, a handful of schools were being given the chance to inaugurate a self-governing program of school-based management. The parents and principal at Garrett Heights were determined to make our school one of those in 1991.

There was good reason for caution, however. When school bells rang, we discovered overcrowded classes. The three mixed-age first/second grade developmental classes had an average of 30 pupils per class. Furthermore, there were no teacher aides except in the prekindergarten class, and, aside from "hard-core" parent group members, few parents were willing to assume this role. Overcrowding, of course, is potentially a problem in any classroom, but especially so in a developmentally appropriate program where children are

not confined to desks, raising their hands and all being taught the same thing at the same time. And, to compound these problems, the principal at Garrett Heights—a school with a population of 470 students in traditional as well as developmental classes—had no assistant principal to help manage it all.

Shortages and lack of resources are not endemic to Garrett Heights, of course. They are typical of any classroom in almost any low-income, urban public school system throughout America. Perhaps this circumstance helps explain the difficulties our Parent Education Group has had in winning its battles to establish developmentally appropriate practice in Baltimore classrooms.

In 1989, there were 99,500 students enrolled in Baltimore City Public Schools (BCPS). For the 1989–90 school year, $4,215 was spent per pupil in Baltimore, compared to $5,497 in neighboring Howard County and $5,177 in surrounding Baltimore County. There is only one computer for every 77.7 children, and the city spends $2.67 per pupil on library books and supplies, compared with Howard County's $17.95. In addition, Baltimore teachers are paid considerably less than teachers with the same experience who work in more affluent counties.

The larger socioeconomic facts are even more telling. Baltimore City schools have one of the highest dropout rates in the country. The city is also distinguished by the largest number of teenage pregnancies of any American city. It has a population of 720,100, and estimates show that up to 200,000 adults in this city are illiterate. Last year, only 67.3% of Baltimore's ninth graders passed the state writing test.

Baltimore boasts the highest property taxes in the state, as well as some of its poorest citizens. New census figures indicate a dramatic population shift away from the city. There are scant financial resources to pump into the school system. There is also a lack of political resolve to force a more equitable distribution of state funding for impoverished school districts.

In the late 1970s and early 1980s, Baltimore was governed by a mayor who successfully rehabilitated the city's downtown area, making it a draw for businesses and tourists. The "renaissance" of Baltimore may have made it a more appealing place to live, but not, unfortunately, to learn. When William Donald Schaefer was elected governor of Maryland in 1987, it was generally acknowledged that his so-called remaking of Baltimore was accomplished without an accompanying improvement in the city schools. (Unfortunately, few cities can claim that renovating the school system has been a fully funded priority, so Baltimore is not alone in this regard.)

In addition, the BCPS school administration has been perceived for years as a muddled bureaucracy, top-heavy with chiefs guarding their political turf. Educational reforms would be initiated and then never followed through, or terminated. Upper- and middle-class—and even working-class parents who can afford it—send their children to private or parochial schools. There had been, and continues to be, a hemorrhage of middle-class families moving from the impoverished city school system to surrounding wealthier counties. (All of this is quite familiar to those who know big cities.) Against this backdrop, when a new mayor was elected in 1987, he vowed to make Baltimore "the city that reads."

Becoming organized

These facts were all known to three friends, parents of preschool children, who got together in the fall of 1987 to talk about schools. They decided that one or two people could not do much to combat the perceived problems, so they got on the telephone and talked to other parents—mostly acquaintances or parents of children they knew from their Waverly neighborhood in northeast Baltimore—and organized a meeting.

About 12 people showed up for that first meeting. Helen Atkinson recalls the tone of that gathering. "We had no focus except a general anxiety. We were all appalled by the same things, and it took many months to get a focus about what we wanted for our children."

What we wanted seemed simple enough. Most of the schools we had visited or learned about did not even offer children a recess. It seemed that the students were small "learning machines," subject to strict timelines in their mastery of classwork and given difficult, academic homework assignments from the beginning of their kindergarten year. The approach to education was rigid and traditional and offered no accommodation to children's individuality.

"The four- and five-year-olds were sitting in a circle working on sight words," says Pat Halle, who visited various elementary schools to see what would be best for her young daughter. "There was a rigid schedule of academic activities. The children were bored, restless, and uninspired. The method of teaching seemed to be about breaking the spirits of the children rather than developing their strengths."

At these early meetings, we instinctively believed that this was the wrong approach. We disagreed with the BCPS theory that the earlier children learn to read, write, and do sums, the better they will be prepared for the future; we even suspected that the result might be just the opposite. Was it possible that one of the reasons so many youngsters drop out of school by ninth grade is because they are burned out and turned off by such an inflexible approach to early childhood education?

We agreed that we shared a commitment to public education and more than a few values, ideas, and priorities. We also agreed to keep meeting and to delegate "fact-finding forays" among ourselves. We made a conscious effort to keep our group democratic, to make decisions based on consensus, and to reach out to other parents.

We were fortunate to have among us Becky Thomson and Jay Gillen, both of whom have backgrounds in education. They became our "experts," consulted at every step. Other parents possessed the skills that would eventually be needed as writers, lobbyists, speakers, and organizers.

In autumn of 1987 and winter of 1988, parents fanned out to interview educators and community organizers and to visit public and private schools. We divvied up books and articles on educational issues. Becky Thomson introduced us to the concept of developmentally appropriate practice (DAP), thus giving a name to the ideas we had been discussing at our group meetings.

Some of the parents had contacts with university educators and early childhood teachers. Community experts in education received telephone calls and visits from group members seeking advice. Alma Cripps and Gail Haldeman, who had taught in an abandoned public school "alternative classroom" using developmentally appropriate practice, counseled us about what a DAP classroom should look like and answered hundreds of questions. Observations at a handful of private schools revealed how such techniques translated into classroom success.

Each finding, each interview, each piece of advice was reported back to parents at group meetings. These meetings were generally organized by parents Helen Atkinson and Pat Halle, who also established the first agendas. They were soon joined by Becky Thomson and Jay Gillen, and later by Malissa Ruffner. This group became a very loose and informal steering committee that kept in touch by telephone between meetings. This democratic structure served its purpose, enabling anyone in the group to take up the leadership role when another left to take a vacation or have a baby. The absence of a single chairperson also kept parents from being overloaded with responsibility and becoming burned out.

During the first year, we met at a neighborhood family support center with which most of us had close ties. Later, meetings were held at individual homes. As the group grew and a school site was selected, the gatherings moved to the more formal setting and smaller chairs of an elementary school library.

Writing a proposal

In December 1987, Jay Gillen drafted our first and most radical proposal. It was primarily influenced by four documents: NAEYC's *Developmentally Appropriate Practice in Early Childhood Programs Serving Children From Birth Through Age 8* by Sue Bredekamp; *Right from the Start* by the National Association of State Boards of Education; "Unacceptable Trends in Kindergarten Entry and Placement," published by the National Association of Early Childhood Specialists in State Departments of Education; and the description of a cooperative learning program in Michigan.

This first draft granted parents powers heretofore unknown in the BCPS system, suggesting that parents devise an appropriate curriculum and participate in planning, budgeting, and hiring processes. Numerous examples of what students would learn were provided, along with the idea that children themselves could help determine curriculum based upon what they said and did in the classroom. Also included was a demand for exemption from standardized testing. In the justification portion of one of our earliest drafts, we wrote "The program would be geared toward both high and low-risk children, and would target families of different racial, economic and educational backgrounds. Rather than focusing on literacy for high-risk students, or accelerated learning for advanced students, the curriculum

would stress the development of social skills, critical thinking, and values in children of all skill levels."

All in all, we prepared ten different drafts of the proposal. Each revision always served two purposes. One was to provide a focal point for the parent group, creating a working document that clarified ideas and merged them as a "mission statement" in which all believed—or at least could live with. The other purpose was persuasion. The working drafts were essentially blueprints that the group planned to submit to BCPS in seeking permission to teach children in an alternative way.

Frequently citing NAEYC journals, we outlined the following envisioned teaching practices: "An emphasis on student initiated activities . . . with children being allowed to select their own work . . . cooperative learning where children would be encouraged to receive help from each other in a mixed age grouping, traditional play-oriented curriculum with children actively handling concrete objects, and thematically integrated projects. By using opportunities throughout the year to learn and practice skills within the context of other skills, children are given repeated opportunity to master each skill, with more complex activities being added."

Early drafts also argued for a kindergarten/first grade class (i.e., a two-year program for five-year-olds), at no expense to the system, open to all who would choose it (within the limits of normal class size). The parent group proposed to raise between $5,000 and $10,000 from private fundraising efforts to cover start-up costs and initial teacher training.

Criteria for teacher selection and specifics of pupil evaluation, however, were deliberately left vague. We were very aware of how even sound educational arguments could flounder in the internecine politics of the BCPS.

Finally, the proposal placed a strong emphasis on parental involvement, adding that there would be no set requirements for parents. A prophetic afterthought concluded, "It will take a lot of work to make this Project a success."

As soon as copies of the proposals were Xeroxed, they were circulated from the hand of one friend to another, placed strategically in the offices of supportive pediatricians, and submitted for revision to education experts and community activists. A cover letter was attached to the proposal, listing Becky Thomson, Helen Atkinson, and Pat Halle as contacts. When people called with questions or to express interest, the contact tried to determine the extent of commitment to public schools represented by the inquiries. Interested individuals were urged to attend the parent meetings. Becky Thomson believes that this circulation process proved to be useful because "it was a good way to recruit new people to the cause."

In the spring of 1988, we named ourselves "The Parent Support Group for the Developmental Classroom." An advisory group was formed consisting of the education professionals who had been informally advising us. In addition, it had become clear that the group needed an interested principal and a school as a focal point for its proposal. And, as ambitions were growing, so was the need to reach out to other parents who could help push the project through to fruition.

Through extensive networking we identified a list of 10 school principals who had reputations as good administrators. Their schools were all within a workable radius of parents' homes. Next, we devised a strategy for approaching them.

"We developed a list of questions," recalls Pat Halle. "So as not to alienate principals or put them on the spot, we agreed to ask hypothetical questions. 'Could this type of program be implemented in a public school? What changes would be needed to make it work within the BCPS system?' Then we quizzed the principal about the strengths and weaknesses of the proposal, finally popping the question: 'Are you interested?' Usually it was clear from the early part of the discussion whether the principal was attuned to developmentally appropriate education."

The list of potential principals and schools was eventually narrowed to three and then one. Billie Rinaldi at Garrett Heights Elementary School was eager, dynamic, and very interested. Her instincts seemed to mesh with the values of the parents, and, just as importantly, she was a savvy veteran of the city school system.

Garrett Heights is a century-old school, located on top of a hill in a working-class neighborhood, very much like the neighborhood where most of the families of the parent group live. It was close to the geographical radius the parents had targeted, and it enjoyed a reputation as an elementary school in which parents were active and involved. There was a mixture of families, approximately 60% White and 40% Black, including families on welfare and lower- and middle-class working parents.

Focusing our efforts, developing our strategy

With a principal and a school targeted, there was finally a focus for our efforts. Autumn of 1988 and winter of 1989 were busy times for our parent support group. Three goals were identified:

• "Sell" the idea of developmentally appropriate practice to the central administration of BCPS to win the go-ahead for implementation.

• Market the concept to parents in the Garrett Heights community who were accustomed to the traditional teaching approach.

• Seek out teachers experienced in developmental practice who might be willing to join our group and work with our children.

BCPS makes all decisions in a centralized manner. Principals, in the overall scheme of things, have very little power and make all but the smallest decisions with the direct approval of their supervisors; therefore, it was not sufficient to have the willingness of Billie Rinaldi to provide a "home" for this program, although she was invaluable in lobbying for approval. Nor did the school board have jurisdiction because it deals primarily with proposals requiring additional funds, which our proposal did not demand. Consequently, we had to seek approval for the Project from the Superintendent of Public Instruction.

Some of our goals were met and others were not. Along the way, certain compromises were made. Making the proposal palatable to school administrators became a top priority; without a nod from them, any reform would be impossible. Subsequent drafts, therefore, gradually deemphasized cooperative learning and emphasized developmentally appropriate practice, which seemed to have more support among mainstream educators. Final drafts downplayed the official role parents would take in hiring and budgeting. On the advice of education activist Joanne Robinson, the group dropped the demand for exemption from standardized testing. Later proposals also avoided curriculum changes, proposing only modifications in teaching techniques and timelines.

According to Pat Halle, "Even though we were arguing for a different way of teaching, we proposed our idea with an understanding of the system's demand for accountability.

We agreed that children taught in this 'alternative' way would be responsible for everything taught 'traditionally' by the time they were in the third grade. We just didn't want them measured at every given point along the way. Testing was and continues to be a sore point for us. We wanted to eliminate it, but were advised by our consultants not to waste our time trying to get exemptions from standardized testing." Also stricken from the final proposal was any perceived criticism of current BCPS practice. The earliest proposal, for example, argued, "The BCPS system loses students to other school systems by not marketing itself to the full range of values in the community." These types of statements were eliminated.

All those advisors who hoped the Project would come to pass contended that such concessions were necessary. Basically, they argued, "BCPS does its own curriculum design, its own hiring, and its own state-mandated testing. Hands off, and you'll have a chance." According to Helen Atkinson, "There was no real bargaining at the end because we had already made the proposal palatable to the BCPS before it went to them."

Although individual parents regretted these concessions, they agreed that the time was not right for such sweeping and drastic departures from current school policy. Having an accepted proposal, albeit a watered-down one, was viewed as a foot in the door. Everyone hoped that once accepted, the Project would be "real," and additional changes could come later.

An approved proposal would also mean accountability. If something agreed upon was not taking place, parents could point to the document and ask, "Why not?" These "giveaways" later frustrated full implementation of the Project, however, especially the deletion of parent involvement in soliciting, interviewing, and hiring trained teachers.

As plans to present the proposal and win agreement from the BCPS went forward, the parent group, with the help of Ms. Rinaldi, planned a large meeting at Garrett Heights in January 1989. The goal was to find out how many parents within the community would be interested in choosing this alternative for their prekindergarten, kindergarten, and first grade children. This was our first attempt to introduce the concepts of developmentally appropriate practice to a larger audience.

Many parents showed up at that January meeting. Some of them had their young children enrolled in schools such as Waldorf, Montessori, or other private institutions. "My wife saw a flyer advertising the meeting at the supermarket," says John Dean, the father of then preschool twins. "We had been sending our children to The Waldorf School, which concentrates on educating 'the whole child.' We wanted to live in the city and send our children to public schools, but we felt that most of them were too harsh in their teaching methods. What we saw in other public schools was an approach that would turn out unquestioning robots, kids who learned how to read but couldn't think for themselves." The majority of parents, however, were unacquainted with developmental practice. Mostly they came because they were interested in quality education for their children.

Ms. Rinaldi explained the differences between a developmental and a traditional classroom. Alma Cripps and Gayle Haldeman, mentors for the parent group as well as veteran developmental teachers, described how children in developmental classes would learn. The new families attending the meeting were enthusiastic and eagerly expressed their interest on a survey circulated by the parent group.

At last, a wider community had been found. There would be students in the developmental classes if the proposal was accepted.

At the next working Parent Support Group meeting, 21 parents, many of them newcomers, were in attendance. They signed up for committees to ready the proposal for BCPS inspection and to investigate fundraising for the Project. Letters were written to the Superintendent of Instruction and his assistants. Arguments were readied, stressing the economy of implementation. Money would be needed only for initial start-up costs, which parents would seek from private foundations.

Letters describing the Project and arguing for its adoption were written by the Parent Support Group. "A helpful image is that of a one-room schoolhouse where the teacher moves among children as their needs dictate and where the older children help their younger classmates . . . . (The school superintendent) has stated that one of his administration's goals is the involvement and mobilization of the community-at-large. We respond to his challenge and feel that the encouragement of well-developed and responsible parent initiatives will be one of the keys to the city's success in the future."

The Parent Support Group found a new ally and Advisory Council member in School Board member Dr. Phillip Farfel, an acquaintance of Billie Rinaldi and a supporter of grassroots efforts. He provided input regarding the proposal and suggested various strategies for its promotion. Roger Lyons of the Baltimore Urban League, JoAnn Carter of the Maryland State Department of Education, and other professionals also wrote letters of support.

Implementing developmentally appropriate practice

By May 18, 1989, it seemed as if all the hard work had paid off. BCPS administrators, after several meetings with Billie Rinaldi and the parents, agreed to the implementation of a three-year project to establish developmentally appropriate classrooms at Garrett Heights. The first year, the program would include a kindergarten and a first grade class. The second year, a second grade class would be added. When an excellent prekindergarten teacher expressed interest, a PreK class was added to the plan.

Feverish work took place during the summer before school began. Grant proposals were written and submitted. In June, the Baltimore-based Fund for Educational Excellence awarded the Parent Support Group a grant for $2,900. Classroom furniture, children's literature books, and hands-on class materials were purchased by, begged for, or borrowed by parents.

Every attempt was made to interest new parents and head off possible resentment of the new program from the Garrett Heights community. "We were concerned that we would be perceived as an elitist group," recalls Becky Thomson, "so we set about joining in all the school activities like picnics and fundraisers. Nevertheless, we were not prepared for the 'turf battle' that occurred when we entered Garrett Heights. Immediately we were thrust into a position of 'us versus them' regarding supplies, fundraising, and attention from the principal." At least six families from the parent group transferred into the Garrett Heights school zone. So not only was the Project new and unfamiliar, so were these non-neighborhood activists.

Trouble brews

A major obstacle to the effort stemmed from our failure to realize an earlier goal. There was a dearth of qualified teachers in a position to teach these new classes. Ms. Rinaldi accompanied several teachers already in place at the school on a tour of the Lida Lee Tall Learning Resource Center, a state-funded elementary school associated with Towson State University and an oasis for developmentally appropriate practice. Only two of the teachers, however, expressed interest in trying to modify their approaches.

Furthermore, the BCPS bureaucracy stymied parental initiatives to help find teachers. "We were told again and again by Billie Rinaldi and her district superintendent that hiring was off-limits. We were flatly told that parents could have no participation in the hiring process," recalls Helen Atkinson about the decision to abandon that demand.

Although an experienced prekindergarten teacher and her aide had been hired early on, it was not until a week before school began that a kindergarten and first grade teacher signed contracts to teach at Garrett Heights. The new kindergarten teacher, who had taught in traditional classrooms, had become disaffected with that approach and was eager to try out developmentally appropriate practice.

The first grade teacher had no real knowledge of developmental teaching and was about to embark on the first job of her career. A veteran second grade teacher was supportive of the approach and helped with a sense of good will among the other traditional teachers. In this first year of the Project, though, she had neither the training nor the experience to fully implement the program in her classroom. We felt frustrated by the fact that the summer, which should have been devoted to training teachers and preparing classrooms, had been wasted.

When the school opened its doors in September 1989, this lack of preparation showed. Although the morning and afternoon prekindergarten classes ran smoothly, illustrating the importance of preplanning, the developmental kindergarten and first grade classes were in trouble from the start.

One large, partitioned room housed two kindergarten classes, one of them traditional and one of them developmental. The first grade was overcrowded. There were 32 students for one inexperienced teacher. The students were strictly assigned by age to their classes, so there was no hope for a scenario whereby "older children would help their younger classmates."

Malissa Ruffner, the parent of a kindergartner in the developmental class, remembers the first four months this way: "The teacher struggled to manage her class, separated from the other kindergarten by only a shoulder-high set of cubbies built by our parent group. Normally, a developmental class is expected to be noisier than a traditional program. But our teacher had to constantly ask the children to be quiet so as not to disturb the traditional class."

By November 1989, Ms. Rinaldi and the parents acknowledged that there were difficulties in all the classes (except the PreK) that threatened to destroy the Project. There was very little about the first grade class that could be described as developmental. Struggling with too many students and suspicious of parent efforts to help, the first grade teacher instructed her children from the blackboard while they remained at their desks. A parent volunteer was scheduled to help in the kindergarten classroom each day, but still the noise from the shared classrooms was deafening, and the teacher grappled with implementing developmental practice. In addition, the central store of consumable supplies was being quickly depleted.

The BCPS attempt in November to ease overcrowding by assigning an extra first grade teacher—yet another novice to the DAP approach—actually exacerbated problems. When the two first grade teachers selected students for their newly configured classrooms, the newest developmental class became a home for the most "challenging" first grade students. The selection process also disregarded parent participation; thus, one classroom enjoyed a high level of parent input while the other class had next to none.

It seemed at times that the Project operated in an environment of constant crisis. According to Malissa Ruffner, "The amount of work was more and more difficult since we were constantly up against someone or something. Our energies, spread out over so many classrooms, dissipated. A surprising development, at least to me, was that approval from the system did not really translate into facilitation. In trying to do something with a completely different atmosphere, every step was like swimming against the current."

Helen Atkinson expressed similar frustration. "The parents had been told at every step that what they wanted was impossible. 'The school system won't allow you to do that.'

'The teachers won't agree to change.' 'Other parents won't agree.' In many ways the nay-sayers were right. Even when we got permission to do something differently, very little changed because some other part of the large bureaucracy couldn't accommodate the exception to the rule, or because staff wasn't available to implement the plan, or because the decision was made so late, there was no time for planning."

But there were small signs of hope

There were, however, small signs of progress within this larger framework—enough to keep the parent group working and hoping. Becky Thomson worked regularly with teachers to help plan their days, arrange their rooms, and develop priorities. She conducted seminars with parents on how to work as classroom aides. As the mother of three children at Garrett Heights, she donated hundreds of hours toward making the two struggling classrooms more developmentally appropriate. For all this she was paid a nominal fee from the grant money.

A parent steering committee worked closely with Ms. Rinaldi in identifying problem areas and in brainstorming solutions. The Advisory Council, which had attracted notable professionals such as the Dean of Early Childhood Education of Towson State University, offered time and resources. Over Christmas break, a new room was found for the developmental kindergarten, and parents hastily moved the contents of the old classroom up a flight of stairs to quieter surroundings. In a letter to the Superintendent of Public Instruction about his visit to the developmental classes, Dr. Phillip Farfel concluded, "Classrooms were filled with excitement and vibrancy as children actively participated in selecting their learning environments. The method was interactive, with many hands-on materials that encouraged children to think and explore."

Indeed, prekindergartners and kindergartners were offered choices of learning activities; for example, children could select building blocks, sand table work, or puzzles. The creation of a classroom restaurant in one of the first grade classes taught students a thematic unit in several subjects from art to vocabulary. One teacher collected a bucket of snow and brought it in for an impromptu science lesson. First graders in one classroom nourished themselves in a private reading loft built by parents and stocked with parent-supplied literature books. Students in all the classrooms "wrote" about their experiences in daily journals as part of a fledgling move toward whole-language instruction.

Another significant victory involved a gradual acceptance of the Developmental Project by parents whose children were in traditional classes. At the year's beginning, many of these families were suspicious and even felt threatened by the creation of an alternative program. In a low-income school system like BCPS, it was perhaps only natural that the addition of a talked-about new program would be viewed as competition for already scarce resources. Unfamiliar with developmentally appropriate classrooms, these parents had perceived the alternative classrooms as "playgrounds" in which very little learning took place.

A number of steps were taken to win the acceptance of these skeptical parents; education was one of them. For example, when Pat Halle heard that DAP author Sue Bredekamp would be in the area, she called and asked her to speak, and then invited the entire school community to hear her lecture. An open house was arranged. Newsletters about DAP were distributed. Fundraising events were coordinated with the Parent-Teacher Group (PTG).

All the parents in the support group worked on the one-on-one human relationships that develop between parents of children who attend the same school. Positive conversations about the Project happened before or after meetings and before or after school, as parents stood together waiting for their children.

Group members were careful never to "demand" special treatment. At a successful meeting held before the kindergarten room change took place, parent representatives from throughout the school listened to each other's concerns and needs. The decision to switch classroom space was made by consensus and took into account the desires of classrooms other than those involved with the Developmental Project.

In the winter of 1990, Becky Thomson and other members of the parent group successfully ran for PTG offices. Although this meant that they could devote less time to the Developmental Project, it also marked a new beginning in schoolwide acceptance. Parents began to notice that recesses, lunchtimes, and even the atmosphere in traditional classrooms were more child-centered as a result of the new leadership. Slowly, the Developmental Project became less isolated from the wider school community as parents with widely divergent views on education learned to work together.

Perhaps the most fundamental change, however, took place in our *expectations*. It became increasingly evident that instituting such radical restructuring was a process, one that would take a great deal of time. Dr. Peter Heaslip, a well-known educator from England, offered some sobering thoughts after conducting a seminar for Garrett Heights teachers in the spring of 1990. "This method of teaching will become a part of the system in Baltimore, and you parents will have been the innovators. But, perhaps, the full realization of this education will not come in time for all your children to benefit."

These were daunting words. A less committed group of parents might merely have walked away, nursing wounds and ruminating on failure. There were, in fact, parents throughout the year who left the group looking for other educational opportunities, safer bets; but there were several key victories that maintained the optimism of most of the activist parents.

More money trickled in to support the program. The Fund for Educational Excellence awarded a $1,500 grant to continue publication of "Developmental Kids," a newsletter published by the parents, and to pay for teacher registration at the 1990 annual NAEYC conference.

Several members of the parent group had been professional fundraisers and successfully acquired a $15,000 grant from the community-based A. S. Abell Foundation. Approved by BCPS administrators, it pays the salary of an experienced trainer/coordinator, Bev Bickel, whose selection was informed by members of the Advisory Council. Her responsibilities include writing a training manual to help other schools establish developmental practice. Now, for the first time, members of the parent group feel free to relax their watchdog role and concentrate on other issues, such as educating parents, fundraising, writing newsletters, and supporting teachers.

Bev Bickel was part of an extremely positive staffing breakthrough. Late in the summer of 1990, two developmental first grade vacancies and a full-time kindergarten position became available. Through timely and extremely effective negotiation, Billie Rinaldi was able to institute a mechanism for hiring experienced and qualified teachers. She was actively supported by the teamwork of the Project's Advisory Council, who helped screen applicants. For the first time, parents, as well as the teacher trainer, were able to participate in the interview process. As a result, three experienced and enthusiastic teachers were offered jobs in the developmental program for the 1990–91 school year.

In addition, new ways to evaluate the program and its students have been instituted. Revamped report cards—with input from the parent steering committee and drafted by the team of teachers with the support of Becky Thomson—are now used with developmental students. The report cards include space for teacher comments and developmentally appropriate checklists for areas such as "Social Relationships" and "Is Growing in Self-Confidence." The report cards also include criteria for "Work Habits and Skills," "Works Well Independently," "Literature Abilities," "Expresses Curiosity," "Composition," and "Has Begun to Write Own Stories." These report cards tell parents much more about their child's progress than standard reports used throughout the BCPS system. "In retrospect," according to Becky Thomson, "this was the easiest change the Project ever accomplished."

The program's evaluation has also been redesigned to be in compliance with the requirements of the A. S. Abell grant. Area university students will conduct pre- and postevaluations of the pupils' progress in reading and language development. These individual assessments will then be compared with a control group. The rigid, standardized testing conducted by the BCPS and required by the state is a major issue this year, but parents, principal, and teachers feel united and strong in their resolve to fight inappropriate testing.

Teachers themselves chose to implement a major goal of the parent group this year: mixed-age classes. There are three first/second grade classrooms in the developmental program. Although there are no formal ways to measure such things, it is clear to observers that kindergartners (now first grade pupils) who graduated from the most developmentally successful class of 1988–89 are coping better with the choices given them in this year's mixed-age developmental classes. In some intangible way, they seem to be adjusting better than second graders (last year's first grade students), who experienced less freedom.

We are not there yet

Still, there are many challenges remaining. A more systematic way to involve the Advisory Council in major issues, such as teacher hiring, needs to be devised. More parents need to be coaxed into giving their time and talent not just to the Developmental Project but also to the school and to the system. The issue of how and when to test students still needs resolving. Overcrowded classrooms must be made smaller. Legislative support for an equalized system of school funding statewide must be sought.

The parent group plans to fight for the addition of more developmental classes at Garrett Heights and throughout the BCPS. Indeed, school administrators now in the process of making the systemwide curriculum more developmentally appropriate need to be educated in order to support the process.

We have learned quite a lot

What lessons can be learned from the long hours we've invested in this process?

1. Form a strong core group of three to five very committed people who share responsibility for leadership. They need to talk with each other a lot and give each other personal support when things look bleak.

2. Learn to call people "in the know" and ask their advice. Make contacts with "friendly" people in power. Start with one or two names and go from there. Pave the way for each request or demand.

3. Be willing to stick your necks out and demand that something be done even when you're told it's impossible. Although this didn't always work, we earned a reputation as a force to be contended with.

4. It is absolutely key to have teachers with energy, commitment, and the ability to adapt and learn. No amount of parent effort can make up for unwilling or unskilled teachers.

5. Have a coordinator, such as Bev Bickel, because this person can do things parents can't in relation to teachers and curriculum. Parents can push for things to happen, but they can't, for example, actually train teachers.

On a more personal level, Malissa Ruffner relates, "It was an incredible outlet for me and taught me as much about politics and strategies for change as it did about kindergarten." According to Marianne Auerweck, "When I chose developmental kindergarten for my son, I thought parent involvement was a prerequisite. I'm so glad I was in the class every week last year because I learned things about him and his education he could never tell me." And Pat Halle reveals, "My involvement taught me to think boldly and broadly about education and the future, not just for my own child, but for all children."

And what of the children? What have they learned? The nearly 200 students, who by the third grade will have been exposed to developmentally appropriate teaching practice at Garrett Heights, cannot be expected to issue a report card of its success; yet someday soon they will speak for themselves. We hope they will be students who love to read, enjoy writing to express themselves, and translate the worlds of math and science in ways that can better humankind. We also hope they will be critical thinkers who are self-confident. Speaking of the aspirations and success of the late Sammy Davis, Jr., Jesse Jackson said, "He never went to school, so he never learned he couldn't." It is imperative that our children learn the most important lesson from their early school experience, and that lesson is, "We can!"

Postscript . . . one year later

The parents who built the Garrett Heights Developmental Classroom Project were less alone during the 1990–91 school year, and that fact may well be the single largest victory of all our efforts. If success can be measured in terms of shaking up the system, creating a dialogue, and planting the seeds for change, then the past year has been a good one.

According to Becky Thomson, "The most significant thing that's happened is parents' changing perceptions of what education means." Increasing numbers of parents began talking about quality education, even if they resisted labels such as "developmentally appropriate."

Teacher empowerment and teacher advocacy for the project went a long way toward the year's successes. As teachers became more proficient with developmentally appropriate practices, they provided examples of what a nonbasic skills approach could accomplish. This freed parent organizers from the role of classroom monitors and transformed the Developmental Classroom Project from a parent-run to a teacher-run project.

Relieved by this positive change, parents felt obligated to support a teacher vote at the end of the school year to eliminate mixed-age classes for the 1991–92 year. Although everyone recognized the advantages of mixed-age classes, there was no denying the mental and physical toll they exacted from teachers who struggled daily to provide individualized experiences for large groups of children with a wide range of abilities.

Another major change has been the Project's gradual integration into the wider school community. Garrett Heights was chosen to be one of a handful of restructured schools in the city school system. A majority of the parents elected to the School Restructuring Team are from the Developmental Classroom Project. In describing their working relationships with other members, Pat Halle explained, "I think we had to let go of distinctions and work hand in hand with the rest of the school. Arguments centered on 'developmental versus traditional' frequently hinder our efforts." So far, the Restructuring Team has adopted a child-centered philosophy.

The Parent-Teacher Group (PTG), headed by Becky Thomson, continues to address issues of quality education with the help of parents from the Developmental Project. The Parent Support Group recently voted to disband and regroup as an education committee under the PTG, working on parent education and schoolwide strategy. According to one parent, "It was useful to have a label and philosophy for everybody to hang a hat on, but it was increasingly difficult to maintain the energy as separate parents devoted to a separate agenda. I think we now have a new direction as a school."

At least two other schools have aligned themselves in partnership with Garrett Heights to raise funds for burgeoning developmentally appropriate programs. The new Baltimore City Public Schools curriculum, revised for the fall of 1991, reflects this approach to learning, as do statewide tests implemented during the past year that emphasize critical thinking rather than memorization.

Finally, at the request of the A. S. Abell Foundation—a major funding source for the Developmental Project—educators from Johns Hopkins University analyzed the results of a test administered to students in Garrett Heights' developmental and corresponding traditional classrooms. Findings regarding students' writing abilities show that children in the Developmental Program write more fluently for a longer period of time than those children in traditional classes.

A measure of children's self-esteem is being scrutinized even more closely. Early results indicated that feelings of self-esteem regarding one's learning skills were about the same among first and second graders at the beginning of the school year. At the end of the school year, however, there were significant differences. Children in the developmental classrooms had much more positive feelings about their academic ability than those in traditional classrooms.

These findings may turn out to be the hard data we have sought in order to prove to others the value of our philosophy. Of course, these results are no surprise to those of us who have been watching these classes throughout the year.

Suggested reading for parents

Ashton-Warner, S. (1963). *Teacher.* New York: Simon & Schuster.

Bredekamp, S. (Ed.). (1987). *Developmentally appropriate practice in early childhood programs serving children from birth through age 8* (exp. ed.). Washington, DC: National Association for the Education of Young Children.

Garrett Heights classroom proposal. (1989, May). [This is the proposal that "started it all." Copies may be requested from Helen Atkinson, 810 Gousuch Avenue, Baltimore, MD 21218. Please send $5.00 to cover the costs of printing and mailing.]

Gatto, J. T. (1990, January). Presentation delivered at the New York State Senate upon receipt of award as the New York City Teacher of the Year. [Copies may be requested from the author at 235 W. 78th Street, New York, NY 10023.]

National Association of State Boards of Education. (1988). *Right from the start.* Alexandria, VA: Author.

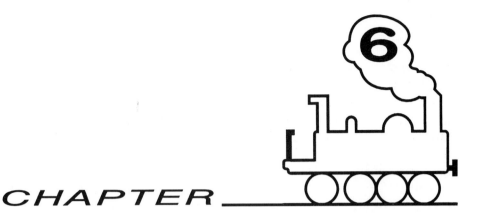

CHAPTER

Challenging the Status Quo: Serving as Critical Change Agents

Stacie G. Goffin

Interest in transforming existing practices in public school early childhood programs is very high, but as each of our authors discloses, awareness of the difficulties inherent in a complex change process often doesn't surface until after one is already immersed in change. Schultz (in press) recently assessed the possibility of integrating developmentally appropriate practice (DAP) in public schools and identified six inhibitors to its quick and universal implementation:

1. the size and complexity of the public education system;

2. the complexity of decision making;

3. the scope of changes required in implementing DAP;

4. the current policy focus on accountability;

5. the shifting, never-ending demands placed upon the education system, making it difficult for schools to focus on any one agenda; and

6. the competing ideas and "packages of curriculum" promoted for early childhood education.

Our authors, however, chose not to be daunted by these barriers. They chose instead to cross that critical, transforming step from concern to action (Goffin & Lombardi, 1988), and, in doing so, they became agents for change.

Their actions, individually and collectively, have enabled more children and teachers to experience the benefits of developmentally appropriate practice and more adults to experience the power (and frustrations) of being early childhood advocates. Although more refined implications can be deduced from these four stories, their most powerful message is that advocates on behalf of developmentally appropriate practice *can* make a difference.

The stories of Emily, Nancy, Larry, and The Parent Support Group portray both the individuality and commonalities of serving as agents for change. Their own stories, of course, best reveal individual differences in position, available resources, and characteristics of the schools and communities that provided the impetus for change and the boundaries for procuring it. The intent of this concluding chapter, therefore, is to identify some common threads that might be informative for others willing to cross over into early childhood advocacy.

Becoming an early childhood advocate on behalf of developmentally appropriate practice, however, requires recognizing that the individuality of these stories about change is, in fact, a commonality. The four stories presented in this book suggest that there is no one way to best effect change in the public schools. This understanding is vital because it empowers all of us to act for change. There are no elusive qualities characteristic of these successful advocates that the rest of us do not already possess or cannot learn. Although their stories highlight the amount of hard work and commitment that making a difference can require, their stories are inspirational and, ultimately, optimistic because they confirm for each of us the possibility of change.

Learning from experience

The experiences of Emily, Nancy, Larry, and The Parent Support Group are also instructive. Despite the variability of their circumstances, certain attitudes and strategies emerge as necessary accompaniments to successfully promoting developmentally appropriate practice in public school settings.

As exemplified by the resounding conclusion of *The Little Engine That Could,* "I think I can! I think I can! . . . I thought I could!" (Piper, 1954), these early childhood advocates were persistent. They never gave up. Although their narratives have been condensed to fewer than 30 pages each, their stories have stretched on for years. Furthermore, these advocates are still at work. As expressed by Larry, "My story of implementing developmentally appropriate practice is still being written."

Still, these advocates knew the endpoint: more developmentally appropriate practices in their public school kindergartens. Many changes were needed to make their early childhood programs more appropriate, and these advocates seized chances to make these changes whenever and however opportunities surfaced.

Even though their commitment to effecting change was often frustrating and emotionally draining, one also senses the exhilaration that comes from being part of something that is really worthwhile. Nancy even concludes that it's been one of the most exciting professional experiences of her life.

None of them, however, anticipated the amount of effort, emotional commitment, and political savvy that would be required of them. Linnea perhaps says it most dramatically. "Setbacks have been the norm rather than the exception . . . . We have become activists who understand that change, especially change within a large bureaucratic institution, does not come overnight. Rather, it comes in incremental doses, a victory here and there within a context of wider, systemic problems." These victories became more than markers of success; they were also critical to maintaining enthusiasm and sustaining hope in the possibility of change.

A critical juncture in preserving individual commitment appeared to occur when, especially as parents and teachers, there was a realization that the effects of their efforts transcended their own classrooms and concern for their own children . . . when they became advocates for everyone's children, not just their own. For Emily, this altered view occurred when her focus extended beyond being "a good teacher" to recognizing herself as a force for change. For the Parent Support Group, this insight occurred when they were forced to confront that the changes they were instigating might not be in place in time to benefit their own children. This realization is perhaps an essential element of any long-term commitment to advocacy.

The willingness and ability to learn from experience would appear to be another critical element of effective advocacy. Each author speaks to what has been learned from being an early childhood advocate. This stance seems important for several reasons. As Nancy relates, "I've learned that you don't have to know it all before getting started; you do, however, have to be willing to take risks and to be imperfect." Without this willingness to take risks and to be imperfect, one could continuously postpone entry into early childhood advocacy because there will always be unknowns.

In addition, early childhood advocates with this perspective are more likely to remain flexible and responsive to unanticipated openings for promoting developmentally appropriate practice. The process of change usually does not occur in a linear or sequential fashion. Lack of flexibility or rigid "game plans" can hinder one's sensitivity to unexpected opportunities to effect change.

In fact, what the stories of Emily, Nancy, Larry, and the parents reveal is the impossibility of "knowing it all" because the process is so fluid and embedded in such complex systems. These advocates, however, quickly learned to rely upon others, as well as themselves, in order to know more. This outreach occurred on two levels. On one level, Emily, Nancy, and members of the Parent Support Group connected with their peers. In this way, they created support systems that helped confirm the validity of their concerns, sustain their involvement, and nurture their optimism.

On another level, they accessed community and professional resources to assist them in accomplishing their goals. Everyone used professional documents and individuals to help validate their concerns and to remove the possibility of inappropriate kindergarten education being minimized as an issue of concern for only a single individual. Emily, Nancy, and the parents also effectively recruited others to place their ideas before decision makers with whom they lacked direct access.

These early childhood advocates made important differences in large part because they succeeded in getting others to join with them in promoting developmentally appropriate practice. Along with others, they exerted focused, extended leadership that maintained visibility for their issue and encouraged significant decision makers and others to address it.

These early childhood advocates, however, did not necessarily enact the same role or perform with the same intensity throughout the life span of their advocacy efforts. Depending upon their interests and the changing circumstances of their personal and professional lives, the type and extent of their involvement shifted. Doing this may have been the reason these advocates were able to remain committed and involved while avoiding burnout. Role shifting was possible, in part, because they had brought others along with them. As Emily's and Nancy's stories reveal, though, there will be times when advocates wish to move on to different issues. To the extent that other advocates share their commitment, this aspect of an effort's evolution can occur with limited disruption.

An intriguing finding from these stories is that the starting point for influencing school practices did not appear particularly significant. All of these authors, regardless of position and first steps as advocates, have made a difference in their public school systems. Furthermore, regardless of the source of the advocacy initiative—principal, superintendent, teacher, or parent—collaboration among all four eventually became necessary. The superintendent level, however, might be unique in its ability to create an educational environment that encourages and nurtures parents, teachers, and principals as advocates for improved learning environments for children.

Emily, Nancy, and Larry, however, probably could have better accessed their "parent power." Their perspectives on parents as collaborators appeared limited to attaining parental support for developmentally appropriate practice, which primarily occurred through attempts at parent education. As the story of The Parent Support Group dramatically illustrates, however, parents can collaborate in ways that extend far beyond acceptance of new school practices. As these parent authors authenticate, parents can be pivotal players in demanding developmentally appropriate practices for children.

The eventual participation of parents, teachers, principals, and administrative staff in achieving developmentally appropriate practice suggests not only that education might be the ultimate collaborative venture but that the changes needed for implementing developmentally appropriate practice in the public schools are both individual and systemic. The necessary resources and support must be forthcoming from all those participating in the education of young children. Early childhood advocates, therefore, will need to try to effect change at multiple levels if the changes they hope to instigate are to be more than transitory and are to extend beyond individual buildings and classrooms.

Placing our advocacy efforts in perspective

The efforts described in this book are part of a long tradition. Conflict between child-centered and instructional approaches to kindergarten education has a history extending back to the first public school kindergarten (Pratt, 1948/1990; Spodek, 1982; Hill, 1987; White & Buka, 1987; Mitchell, Seligson, & Marx, 1989). Susan Blow (who implemented the first public school kindergarten in St. Louis in 1871) expressed concern to her superintendent that the freedom children enjoyed in kindergarten made transitions to regular school classrooms difficult (Osborn, 1980). And, in 1908, Benjamin Gregory wrote the following:

In passing from the kindergarten to the primary school, there is a break. Do what you will to soften the change, to modify the break, it still remains a break. Three general methods of dealing with the difficulty have been employed: (1) To provide a connecting class to take the child out of his kindergarten habits and introduce him to those of the primary school; in the words of some teachers, "to make him over." (2) To modify the kindergarten and make it more nearly resemble the primary schools. (3) To modify the primary school to make it more nearly resemble the kindergarten. (p. 22)

In contemporary terms, Gregory's first option would probably be labeled transitional first grade. The second option, of course, is the pervasive situation that Emily, Nancy, Larry, and The Parent Support Group are attempting to deflect. Based upon their successes, the third option still seems possible.

Their efforts have influenced the learning environments not only of kindergartens but also of first and second grades. Their efforts have successfully modified primary schools to make them more nearly resemble the kindergarten. As stated by Larry, whose conclusion is especially encouraging because of his position as a school superintendent, "Appropriate practices are appropriate practices regardless of the age of the child."

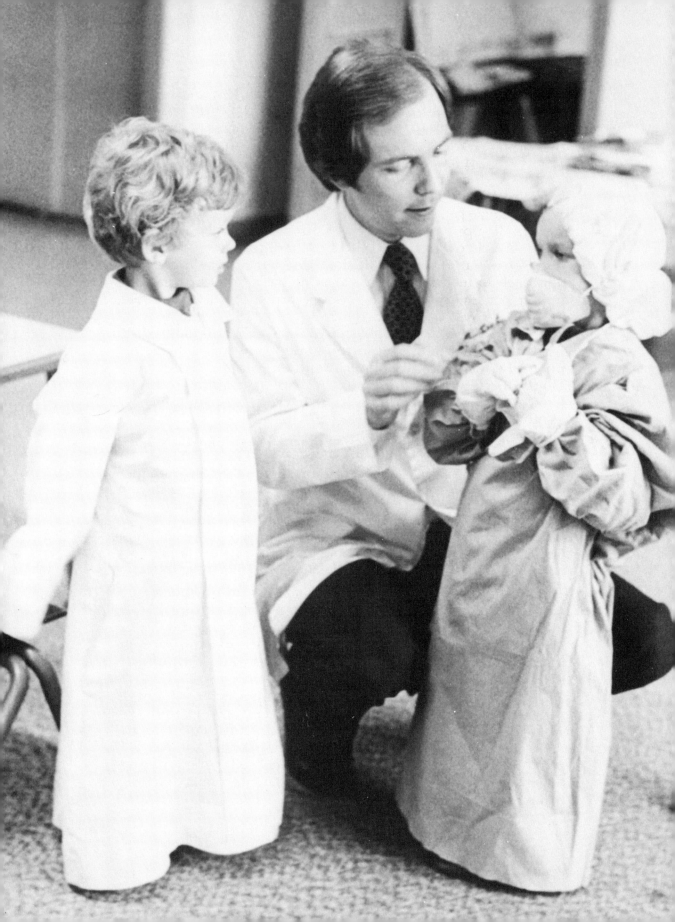

Cautious optimism also seems reasonable because of the recent support being offered by a diverse array of national organizations, including the National Association for the Education of Young Children (Bredekamp, 1987), National Association of Elementary School Principals (1990), the National Education Association (NEA) (1990), and the National Association of State Boards of Education (1988). Each of these groups has endorsed the importance of developmentally appropriate practice for children through the early primary grades.

These endorsements suggest a changing context for securing developmentally appropriate practice in public schools. They imply a widening window of opportunity for early childhood advocates seeking to implement more appropriate learning opportunities for young children. The effort being made by the Missouri State Department of Elementary and Secondary Education, which Nancy briefly describes, is a significant example of one such opportunity.

In a 1926 article discussing the schism between kindergarten and the primary grades, Patty Smith Hill wrote,

Fortunately for children as well as teachers, this whole situation has changed. Kindergarten and primary teachers are trained in the same teacher education programs with the same psychology and philosophy, the same materials and methods . . . . Kindergarten and primary teachers are cooperating in the construction of a unified curriculum in which the activities, subjects, and materials of the kindergarten are traced on up to the second, third, or fourth grade. (Hill, 1987, p. 14)

The efforts of Emily, Nancy, Larry, and the parent members involved with the Developmental Classroom Project have enabled early childhood classrooms in their communities to become more developmentally appropriate for children and teachers. Through their efforts, and those of other early childhood advocates throughout the states, Hill's vision may yet come true.

References

Bredekamp, S. (Ed.). (1987). *Developmentally appropriate practice in early childhood programs serving children from birth through age 8* (exp. ed.). Washington, DC: National Association for the Education of Young Children.

Goffin, S. G., & Lombardi, J. (1988). *Speaking out: Early childhood advocacy.* Washington, DC: National Association for the Education of Young Children.

Gregory, B.C. (1908). The necessity of continuity between the kindergarten and the elementary school: The present status, illogical and unFrobellian. In B. C. Gregory, J. B. Merrill, B. Payne, & M. Giddings (Eds.), *The coordination of the kindergarten and the elementary school,* The Seventh Yearbook of the National Society for the Scientific Study of Education, Part 2 (pp. 22–34). Chicago: University of Chicago Press.

Hill, P. S. (1987). The function of the kindergarten. *Young Children, 42*(5), 12–19. (Original work published 1926)

Mitchell, A., Seligson, M., & Marx, F. (1989). *Early childhood programs and the public schools: Between promise and practice.* Dover, MA: Auburn House.

National Association of Elementary School Principals. (1990). *Early childhood education and the elementary school principal: Standards for quality programs for young children.* Alexandria, VA: Author.

National Association of State Boards of Education. (1988). *Right from the start.* Alexandria, VA: Author.

National Education Association. (1990). *Early childhood education and the public schools.* Washington, DC: Author.

Osborn, D. K. (1980). *Early childhood education in historical perspective.* Athens, GA: Education Associates.

Piper, W. (1954). *The little engine that could.* New York: Platt & Munk.

Pratt, C. (1990). *I learn from children* (First Perennial Library Edition). New York: Harper and Row. (Original work published 1948 by Simon & Schuster)

Schultz, T. (in press). Developmentally appropriate practice and the challenge of public school reform. In D. Stegelin (Ed.), *Early childhood education: Policy issues for the 1990s.* Norwood, NJ: Ablex.

Spodek, B. (1982). The kindergarten: A retrospective and contemporary view. In L. G. Katz (Ed.), *Current topics in early childhood education* (Vol. 4, pp. 173–191). Norwood, NJ: Ablex.

White, S. H., & Buka, S. L. (1987). Early education: Programs, traditions, and policies. In E. Z. Rothkopf (Ed.), *Review of research in education* (Vol. 14, pp. 43–91). Washington, DC: American Educational Research Association.

For Further Reading

More stories by teachers

DeClark, G. (1985). From skepticism to conviction. In C. K. Kamii, *Young children reinvent arithmetic: Implications of Piaget's theory* (pp. 195–202). New York: Teachers College Press.

Divorky, D. (1978). Dorothy Finken: A reborn teacher. *Learning,* 88–90.

Humphrey, S. (1989). Becoming a better kindergarten teacher: The case of myself. *Young Children, 45*(1), 17–22.

Rasola, S. M. (1989). Assignment in kindergarten: Introduce a new curriculum. *Young Children, 43*(5), 60–65.

Understanding the change process

Davis, M. (1989). Preparing teachers for developmentally appropriate classrooms. *Dimensions, 17*(3), 4–7.

Fullan, M. (1982). *The meaning of educational change.* New York: Teachers College Press.

Goffin, S. G. (in press). Creating change with public schools: Reflections of an early childhood teacher educator. In D. Stegelin (Ed.), *Early childhood education: Public policy issues for the 1990s.* Norwood, NJ: Ablex Publishing.

Goffin, S. G. (1991). Supporting change in a school district's early childhood programs: A story of growth. *Early Development and Care 70,* 5–16..

Haskins, G. P., & Alessi, S. J. (1989). An early childhood center developmental model for public school settings. *Teachers College Record, 90,* 415–433.

Hord, S. M., Rutherford, W. L., Huling-Austin, L., & Hall, G. E. (1987). *Taking charge of change.* Alexandria, VA: The Association for Supervision and Curriculum Development.

McDonald, J. P. (1989). When outsiders try to change schools from the inside. *Phi Delta Kappan, 7*(3), 206–212.

Murphy, C. U. (1991). Lessons from a journey into change. *Educational Leadership, 48*(8), 63–67.

Rust, F. O. (1989). Early childhood in public education: Managing change in a changing field. *Teachers College Record, 90*(3), 452–464.

Sarason, S. B. (1982). *The culture of the school and the problem of change* (2nd ed.). Boston: Allyn and Bacon.

Sarason, S. B. (1987). Policy, implementation, and the problem of change. In S. L. Kagan & E. F. Zigler (Eds.), *Early schooling: The national debate* (pp. 116–126). New Haven, CT: Yale University Press.

Schultz, T. (in press). Developmentally appropriate practice and the challenge of public school reform. In D. Stegelin (Ed.), *Early childhood education: Policy issues for the 1990s.* Norwood, NJ: Ablex Publishing.

Walsh, D., Baturka, N., Colter, N., & Smith, M. E. (1991). Changing one's mind—maintaining one's identity: A 1st grade teacher's story. *Teachers College Record, 93,* 73–86.

Waugh, R. F., & Punch, K. F. (1987). Teacher receptivity to systemwide change in the implementation stage. *Review of Educational Research, 57,* 237–254.

Weber, E. (1969). *The kindergarten: Its encounter with educational thought in America.* New York: Teachers College Press.

Advocating for continued change

Bredekamp, S., & Shepard, L. (1989). How best to protect children from inappropriate school expectations, practices, and policies. *Young Children, 43*(3), 14–24.

Elkind, D. (1987). Early childhood education on its own terms. In S. L. Kagan & E. F. Zigler (Eds.), *Early schooling: The national debate* (pp. 98–115). New Haven, CT: Yale University Press.

Goffin, S. G., & Lombardi, J. (1988). *Speaking out: Early childhood advocacy.* Washington, DC: National Association for the Education of Young Children.

Goffin, S. G., & Myers, M. (1989). *A landscape of concerns: A resource reference of position papers.* Washington, DC: National Association for the Education of Young Children.

Kamii, C. (Ed.). (1989). *Achievement testing in the early grades: The games grown-ups play.* Washington, DC: National Association for the Education of Young Children.

Mitchell, A., & Modigliani, K. (1989). Public policy report: Young children in the public schools? The "only ifs" reconsidered. *Young Children, 44*(6), 56–61.

National Association of State Boards of Education. (1988). *Right from the start.* The report of the NASBE Task Force on Early Childhood Education. Alexandria, VA: Author.

Peck, J. T., McCaig, G., & Sapp, M. E. (1988). *Kindergarten policies: What is best for children?* Washington, DC: National Association for the Education of Young Children.

Seefeldt, C., & Barbour, N. (1988). "They said I had to . . . " Working with mandates. *Young Children, (43)*4, 4–8.

Information About NAEYC

NAEYC is. . .

. . .a membership-supported organization of people committed to fostering the growth and development of children from birth through age eight. Membership is open to all who share a desire to serve and act on behalf of the needs and rights of young children.

NAEYC provides. . .

. . .educational services and resources to adults who work with and for children, including
- *Young Children, the* journal for early childhood educators
- **Books, posters, brochures,** and **videos** to expand your knowledge and commitment to young children, with topics including infants, curriculum, research, discipline, teacher education, and parent involvement
- An **Annual Conference** that brings people from all over the country to share their expertise and advocate on behalf of children and families
- **Week of the Young Child** celebrations sponsored by NAEYC Affiliate Groups across the nation to call public attention to the needs and rights of children and families
- **Insurance plans** for individuals and programs
- **Public affairs information** for knowledgeable advocacy efforts at all levels of government and through the media
- The **National Institute for Early Childhood Professional Development,** providing resources and services to improve professional preparation and development of early childhood educators
- The **National Academy of Early Childhood Programs,** a voluntary accreditation system for high-quality programs for children
- The **Information Service,** a centralized source of information sharing, distribution, and collaboration

For free information about membership, publications, or other NAEYC services . . .
- call NAEYC at 202–232–8777 or 800–424–2460
- or write to the National Association for the Education of Young Children, 1509 16th St., N.W., Washington, DC 20036–1426.

More Resources From NAEYC

The second in NAEYC's monograph series!

Kindergarten Policies: What Is Best for Children?
—by *Johanne T. Peck, Ginny McCaig, and Mary Ellen Sapp.*
For decision makers. At what age should children start kindergarten? How useful are entrance tests? What is appropriate kindergarten curriculum? Are full days better than half days? This volume discusses research on these and related issues from the point of view of what is best for children.

This book has helped many schools change their approach!

Developmentally Appropriate Practice in Early Childhood Programs Serving Children From Birth Through Age 8
—*Sue Bredekamp, Editor.* This definitive work is our profession's consensus of what are appropriate and inappropriate teaching practices for infants through eight-year-olds. There are separate chapters on children from birth to age three, three-year-olds, four- and five-year-olds, and five-through eight-year-olds.

The Case for Mixed-Age Grouping in Early Childhood Education—by *Lilian G. Katz, Demetra Evangelou, and Jeanette Allison Hartman.* Are you considering doing mixed-age grouping of your three-, four-, five-, and six-year-olds? What can children gain socially? Cognitively? This book offers suggestions for making mixed-age settings work well and answers many questions you may have.

Achievement Testing in the Early Grades: The Games Grown-Ups Play—*Constance Kamii, Editor.* The trend is to observe and record, and to do much less testing. Grown-ups at all levels involved with teaching and testing in kindergarten and the primary grades need to stop playing the "looking-good game" and consider the facts: The use of norm-referenced testing has gone haywire. Expert theoretician Constance Kamii and a team of concerned professionals explain how test mania does not tell us what we need to know about children's progress, encourages bad teaching, and *harms children.*

The fourth in NAEYC's monograph series!

Beyond Self-Esteem: Developing a Genuine Sense of Human Value—by *Nancy E. Curry and Carl N. Johnson.* What does research say about how young children really develop self-esteem? It's much more than a matter of stickers and indiscriminate praise! For teachers, teacher educators, and others whose behaviors and decisions influence how very young children judge themselves.

The Block Book—*Elisabeth S. Hirsch, Editor.* How well-equipped is your block area? Find out why blocks are a marvelous investment for learning through play.

Young Children and Picture Books: Literature From Infancy to Six—by *Mary Renck Jalongo.* A book every good teacher of young children will want. Reading to young children is in style, but *what* we read to them is important, too. What constitutes high-quality literature and art for children? How do good books benefit children? Find out in this lovely expert discussion.

Woodworking for Young Children—by *Patsy Skeen, Anita Payne Garner, and Sally Cartwright.* Learn a new skill! Find out what woods are easiest to work with, what kinds of hammers and nails are best, and what children can learn. Teach woodworking even if you don't know a thing about it—you soon will!

For a free catalog of these and other NAEYC resources,
- call NAEYC at 202-232-8777 or 800-424-2460
- or write to the National Association for the Education of Young Children, 1509 16th St., N.W., Washington, DC 20036–1426.